worship

searching for language

D0378407

worship

searching for language

Gail ramshaw

The Pastoral Press
Washington, DC

The illustration on the front cover, Secular Teaching Scene, is from a fourteenth century Latin vocabulary book from Admont, Austria, Ms. 368, fol. 1. The female figure sitting on the podium is a Personification of Grammar, one of the Seven Liberal Arts.

ISBN: 0-912405-49-X

© The Pastoral Press, 1988
All Rights Reserved

The Pastoral Press

225 Sheridan Street, NW
Washington, D.C. 20011
(202) 723-1254

The Pastoral Press is the publication division of the National Association of Pastoral Musicians, a membership organization of musicians and clergy dedicated to fostering the art of musical liturgy.

Printed in the United States of America

Acknowledgements

"Literary Images of the Dying Christ." Originally published as "Portraits of the Dying Christ," *Response* 18 (1978) 4–9. "'The Dream of the Rood': A Translation." Originally published as "The Dream of the Rood," *Liturgy* 1 (1980) 10–13. Copyright, The Liturgical Conference, 806 Rhode Island Avenue, N.E., Washington, D.C. 20018. All rights reserved. Used with permission. *"The White Hotel* and the Feast of the Holy Innocents." Originally published as "The Word in the World," *Consensus* 8 (1982) 23–27. Reprinted with permission. "Children's Literature for the Religious Imagination." Originally written for *Lutheran Partners*. Used with permission. "Mary as the Symbol of Grace." Originally published as "Mary and the Paradox of Grace," *Modern Liturgy* 9 (1982) 6–7. Reprinted with permission from *Modern Liturgy*, 160 E. Virginia Street, #290, San Jose, California 95112. "On Meeting Mother Rome." Originally published as "On Meeting Mother," *Dialog* 22 (1983) 43–44. Reprinted with permission. "Typology as Biblical Symbol." Originally published as "Towards Typology Reborn," Sixteenth Lecture of the Robinson T. Orr Visitorship, Huron College, London, Ontario, October 1985. "The Cross and St. Francis." Originally published as "His Sign," Chapter 6 in *Francis: A Saint We Share* (New York: Paulist, 1982) 74–86, publication sponsored by the American Lutheran Publicity Bureau and Graymoor Ecumenical Institute. Reprinted with permission. "C and P." Originally published in *Letters for God's Name* (Minneapolis: Seabury, 1984). "Dancing Around the Burning Bush." Originally published as "Words around the Fire," *Religion and Intellectual Life* 4 (1987) 26–29. Reprinted with permission. "Choosing the Words for the Church." Originally published as "Choosing the Words of the Church," *Word & World* 6 (1986) 288–94. Reprinted with permission. "Blessing God with Bread and Wine." Originally published in *Reformed Liturgy and Music* 19, #1 Winter 1985. Reprinted with permission of the Office of Worship, Presbyterian Church U.S.A. "Teaching Children the Words of Faith." Originally published as "Catechesis for Baptized Children," *Liturgy* 4 (1983) 75–80. Copyright, The Liturgical Conference, 806 Rhode Island Avenue, N.E., Washington, D.C.

20018. All rights reserved. Used with permission. "The Poetic Nature of Liturgical Language." Originally published as "Liturgy as Poetry: Implications of a Definition," *Living Worship* 15:8 (1979). Copyright, The Liturgical Conference, 806 Rhode Island Avenue, N.E., Washington, D.C. 20018. All rights reserved. Used with permission. "The Language of Eucharistic Praying," Originally published in *Worship* 57 (1983) 419–37. Reprinted with permission. "Sin: One Image of Human Limitation." Originally published in *Concilium* 1987/2, pp. 3–10 (Edinburgh, Scotland: T. & T. Clark Ltd., 1987). Reprinted with permission. "Language about God: Muddle and Mystery." Originally published in *Reformed Liturgy and Music* 17, #4 Fall 1983. Reprinted with permission of the Office of Worship, Presbyterian Church U.S.A. "Liturgical Prayer and God as Mother." Originally published as "Lutheran Liturgical Prayer and God as Mother," *Worship* 52 (1978) 517–42. Reprinted with permission. "De Divinis Nominibus: The Gender of God." Originally published in *Worship* 56 (1982) 117–31. Reprinted with permission. "Naming the Trinity: Orthodoxy and Inclusivity." Originally published in *Worship* 60 (1986) 491–98. Reprinted with permission.

with gratitude to Gordon Lathrop

Contents

Introduction

It is both a delight and a mortification to edit past essays for reprinting. There are those pleasant moments of rediscovering something long forgotten. There are little turns of phrase that bring on a smile, even after a decade. But there is also both the dread that it all sounds the same and, paradoxically, the disgust at having declaimed such arcane positions. I have decided to edit not only the gross errors and to retain the progression of thought. Thus some of these essays are based on a theory of metaphor I later rejected, or are marked by a conviction which I no longer hold. I changed, the positions changed.

What did not change is my passion to search for liturgical language, to learn the Scriptures and to read the service books, to study the languages and to examine contemporary speech, to probe for the meaning behind the words, and so to account for the language of the church. I offer these essays back to you, hoping that the evidence of my continuing struggle to know the language of the church will call also you to study and to prayer. I know that one can never know the Name. But one tries. And in the liturgy one discovers a gift of grace: that in the prayers of the church, in the proclamation of the word, in the bread and wine, in the handshake of peace, one has already been embraced by all of the Name that one needs.

LEARNING FROM LITERATURE

1

Literary Images of the Dying Christ

THE UNIQUE NATURE OF EACH OF THE FOUR GOSPELS IS MARKEDLY seen in their passion narratives. Despite the probability of various pre-gospel traditions, each completed narrative offers a distinctive portrait of the dying Christ, and it is not surprising that the four accounts demonstrate the development of Christology in the early church. Written about A.D. 70, Mark's passion narrative presents a passive, suffering victim, rejected by his followers, maligned by his enemies, and finally abandoned by God. Matthew's elaboration of the Markan narrative upholds the weak sufferer with more explicit Old Testament expectations. In Luke, written between A.D. 70 and 90, Jesus is an active participant in his passion, healing, forgiving, and living in obedience to the Father. Lastly, John, written in the 90s, presents the most powerful Christ, who as the Son of God willingly seeks death to achieve life.

These passion narratives have inspired the writing of countless more. Here we will examine the following: Egeria's diary (fifth century); "Vexilla Regis" (ca. 569); "The Dream of the Rood" (ca. 700); the Reproaches (ninth through eleventh centuries); "Stabat Mater" (thirteenth century); "Stond well, moder" (fourteenth century); the Wakefield play on the buffeting (ca. 1410); the York play on the crucifixion (fifteenth century); "Tomorrow will be my dancing day" (sixteenth century); "O Haupt voll Blut und Wunden" (1656), and "When I Survey the Wondrous Cross" (1707). Although the church's pious devotional meditation on the passion, as seen in the Stations of the Cross and Good Friday's Tre Ore service, suggests a focus on a Markan view of Jesus as the suffering victim, it is the Johannine victorious king who reigns over much of the literature of the passion.

Mark

Only one of these literary pieces is particularly Markan: "The Buffeting," from the cycle plays performed in Wakefield, England.[1] The passion plays were originally performed by the monks on Good Friday, but because of their length and increasing secularity, they were taken over by the guilds on Corpus Christi Day. The various plays in the cycle were written by different anonymous authors. "The Buffeting," from about 1410, is an original composition of the "Wakefield Master," the cycle's final editor and the author of the raucous "Second Shepherd's Play." While the Wakefield Master has taken from John the names "Anna" and "Cayphas," the narrative of the Sanhedrin trial is based closely on Mark 14:53–65.

The play begins with an imaginative development of Mark's account of the false witnesses. The two "torturers" combine the various traditions of Jesus' ministry in accusing him of preaching a new law, of being acclaimed "godis son of heuen" (line 91), of telling lies, and of using witchcraft to heal the deaf and dumb and to raise Lazarus. The Markan stress on Jesus' connection with the demons is central to this trial account: "And euer thrugh his soceres oure sabate day defyles" (line 85). The specific accusation in Mark 14:58 appears here:

> Sir, I hard hymn say he cowthe dystroew / our tempyll so gay,
> and sithen beld a new / on the third day. (lines 73–74)

The Wakefield Master cleverly uses the false witnesses to outline for the audience Jesus' life of good deeds.

The silence of Jesus (Mk 14:61) provides the Wakefield Master with comic opportunities. Cayphas becomes an incompetent bully, furious that Jesus will not answer the accusations. Finally Anna subdues Cayphas' diatribes, reminding his son-in-law that

1. "The Buffeting," *The Towneley Plays*, ed. George England (London: Oxford, Early English Text Society, 1966) 228–242.

as "a man of holy kyrk" (line 208) he must refrain from punching Jesus. In the second half of the play, the torturers buffet the silent Jesus, blindfolding him for a game of prophecy, providing slapstick comedy by their antics. In the middle of the play comes Anna's direct question to Jesus:

—Say, art thou godys son of heuen,
  As thou art wonte for to neuen?   (relate)
—So thou says by thy steuen,   (voice)
  and right so I am;
  ffor after this shall thou se / when that I do come downe
  in brightnes on he/ in clowdys from abone. (lines 249–54)

Except for the identification of Jesus as the Son of Man, this is the Markan account. First is the bickering of the false witnesses, second the maligned and mistreated Jesus and his eschatological response, lastly the buffeting. The Wakefield Master shows Jesus as the victim, abused and abandoned.

Matthew

The Matthean passion narrative is close to the Markan, but here is a stronger Christ, described as messiah by the Old Testament Scriptures and acclaimed Lord by the writer's church. With the Scriptures and the church to support the writer, Jesus is not quite the abandoned victim that Mark portrays. It is this Matthean Jesus which inspired the portrait of Christ in Jerusalem's fifth century Good Friday ritual as described by the pilgrim nun Egeria.[2]

The Holy Week liturgy was a series of vigils conducted at appropriate locations around Jerusalem: on Friday Gethsemane, Pilate's courtyard, Golgotha, and the Holy Sepulcher were visited. In each place the applicable passages were read from the psalms, the prophets, the epistles, and the gospels. Scripture was selected to focus on the suffering Christ—a Matthean emphasis. The purpose of this rite was to become overwhelmed with sorrow at Christ's sufferings. Egeria writes:

2. *Egeria: Diary of a Pilgrimage,* ed. George Gingras (New York: Newman, 1970).

> During the reading of this passage there is such moaning and groaning with weeping from all the people that their moaning can be heard practically as far as the city. (p. 109)

Further:

> At each reading and at every prayer, it is astonishing how much emotion and groaning there is from all the people. There is no one, young or old, who on this day does not sob more than can be imagined for the whole three hours, because the Lord suffered all this for us. (p. 112)

The Golgotha ritual included the adoration of the relic of the true cross, thus emphasizing the sufferings of the dying Christ rather than his salvific power; and one need only speculate on the emotional condition of these exhausted and fasting pilgrims to imagine the devotional piety these rites achieved. This rite and its popular descendant, the Way of the Cross, ground the sorrows of the dying Lord in the biblical witness just as Matthew finds the basis of his narrative in the Scriptures of his people.

"Stabat Mater" is a hymn ascribed to Jacopone da Todi in the thirteenth century.[3] Appointed for use especially on the Friday after Passion Sunday, this hymn enjoyed great popularity in medieval piety and heavily influenced the church's portrait of the dying Christ. "Stabat Mater" is a hymn to and about the Virgin, not Christ, and thus is a development of church tradition rather than a use of the gospel narratives.

Although only John places Mary at the foot of the cross, neither the Mary nor the Jesus of the "Stabat Mater" are Johannine; for Mary is sobbing disconsolately and her son dying weakly. While Mary is somewhat Lukan, the son is a Matthean Christ. Stanzas two and three state that Mary sorrows both with and for her suffering son, and stanza four quotes Matthew in the description of Jesus. It was *pro peccatis suae gentis* (Mt 1:21) that he suffers. She watches him, *moriendo desolatum* until *emisit spiritum* (Mt 27:50). This focus on the suffering Christ is an extension of the rites Egeria described, in which Christ as victim is acclaimed as

3. "Stabat Mater," *The Hymns of the Breviary and Missal*, ed. Matthew Britt (New York: Benziger, 1922) 132–133.

Lord through his pain. Never in the ten stanzas does Jesus respond to Mary, as he would in a Lukan picture.

Luke

Luke makes a distinctive contribution to the portrait of the dying Christ. All through Luke's passion narrative Jesus remains an active participant, a healing savior for all. He is strengthened by the angel for his passion; he heals the soldier's ear; he looks on Peter; he effects Herod's and Pilate's reconciliation; he comforts the weeping women, forgives the soldiers and the dying thief, and offers himself to his Father. In nearly every scene he acts to save his people, and this passion tradition in liturgical piety adds the savior to the victim, heightening the theology of the crucifixion scene.

The anonymous Middle English lyric from the early fourteenth century, "Stond well, moder, under rode," corresponds to Luke's portrait of the dying Christ.[4] Although the specific tableau is Johannine, with the mother of Jesus at the cross, Christ is a Lukan suffering and forgiving savior. Mary describes his suffering:

I see thin fet, I see thin honde
Nailed to the harde tree . . .

I see the blody stremes erne   (flow)
from this herte to my fet. (lines 5–6, 23–24)

But the son is comforting his mother.

Moder, now I may thee seye:
Betere is that ich one deye
Than all monkunde to hell go. (lines 25–27)

The sinful history of the race, the virgin birth, and the resurrection ("The thridde day I rise upon") are recited, and, just as for the Lukan tradition, God's actions unfold in history. The dialogical nature of the lyric reflects Luke's interacting savior.

4. "Stond well, moder," *Middle English Lyrics*, ed. Maxwell S. Luria and Richard L. Hoffman (New York: W. W. Norton, 1974) 215–217.

Luke's report of the repentant thief is perhaps the inspiration for the poem's last stanzas, in which Christ's death is directly connected with the gift of heaven for the sinner:

> Blessing be thou, full of blisse!
> Let us never hevene misse,
> Thourgh thy swete sones might. (lines 61–63)

Although Christ is suffering, his suffering brings salvation, both in Luke and in this lyric.

The cycle plays of York, England, had a master editor in the early fifteenth century. Called the "York Realist," this editor wrote "The Crucifixion" in alliterative verse descendant from Anglo-Saxon conventions and in twelve-line rhyming stanzas.[5] The York play was performed by the guild of pin-makers, and appropriately one-third of the play deals with the four soldiers' difficulties with the nails and nailholes. Speaking all but two of the twenty-five stanzas, the soldiers hold Jesus down, complain about the misplaced nailholes, nail Jesus to the cross, carry it up Calvary's hill with many complaints about their exhaustion, drop the cross in the hole, and throw dice for the cloak. The play is remarkably realistic in depicting four professionals doing a day's work.

Although the soldiers generally ignore Jesus, they call him names: "dote" (fool), "traitor," "faitour" (faker), "cursed knave," "lad," and "harlot" (rascal). The Markan theme recurs, asserting that Jesus is bewitched, a "warlock" who commits "gauds" and "cautels" (tricks). But the Lukan portrait takes over as the soldiers discuss Jesus' claim of kingship (Lk 23:2) and mock his messianic title (Lk 23:36–37) in spite of his forgiving nature:

> 1. We! hark! he jangles like a jay.
> 2. Methink he patters like a pie.
> 3. He has been doing so all day,
>   And made great moving of mercy.
> 4. Is this the same that gan us say
>   That he was God's Son almighty? (lines 265–270)

---

5. "The Crucifixion," *Everyman and Medieval Miracle Plays*, ed. A. C. Cawley (New York: E. P. Dutton, 1959) 143–155.

Jesus speaks two of the stanzas. In his first speech he prays to his Father that "from that sin for to save mankind," "they for me may favour find / And from the fiend them fend" (lines 54, 56–57). The prayer is one of obedience to the Father's will and for the salvation of the people. His second speech is based on Lamentations 1:12 and Luke 23:24, as Jesus proclaims his sufferings as salvific for all and prays for the soldiers who crucify him. Here the Lukan Jesus is already saving his people.

Although J.S. Bach incorporated the chorale "O Haupt voll Blut und Wunden" into his *St. Matthew Passion*, the portrait of Jesus in the text is Lukan.[6] The hymn, written by the Lutheran Paul Gerhardt in 1656, is based on the Latin "Salve caput cruentatum," attributed to Bernard of Clairvaux. The first three stanzas of the German hymn focus on the sufferings of the noble Christ:

> O Haupt voll Blut und Wunden,
> Voll Schmerz und voller Hohn . . .
>
> Wie bist du so bespeit!
> Wie bist du so erbleichet! (lines 1–2, 12–13)

The hymn writer stands in the place of the women in Luke 23:27–31 who mourn Jesus' condition. The stress is on the contrast between his debased appearance, the blood, the crown of thorns, the pale complexion, and his true status as Lord. His head, *sonst schon gezieret / Mit hochster Ehr und Zier* (lines 5–6), is now abused and bleeding. The pale countenance is *edles*. Stanzas four through ten conclude the Lukan picture, for Christ on the cross is the savior, called *Herr, Erbamer, Hüter, Hirte, liebster Freund*, and *Heil*. The look Jesus gives to Peter in Luke 22:61 appears also for the poet:

> Gib mir, O mein Erbarmer,
> Den Anblick deiner Gnad'! (lines 31–32)

The poet joins with the repentant crowds at the cross (Lk 23:48) in stanza six, asking to see *dein Bilde / In deiner Kreuzesnot* (lines 75–76) and by those sufferings to be saved.

6. Paul Gerhardt, "O Haupt voll Blut," *The Handbook to the Lutheran Hymnal*, ed. W. G. Polack, 3rd ed. (St. Louis: Concordia, 1958) 135–136.

John

It is the paradoxes in the Gospel of John which inspire some of the greatest passion poems. The darkness which illuminates, the suffering which is glory, the Son of God who offers his death for life not only provide the poets with specific material but also suggest metaphor—that tension in talking about two different things at once—as the method of picturing the crucifixion. In John, Christ is the conquering hero, powerful enough to accept death, rebuking the soldier, intimidating Pilate, creating Christian community from the cross, and dying that God's will be accomplished. Even the soldiers' mockery of Jesus as a king is in John not pitiful, but rather ironic, for John's narrative asserts that Jesus is indeed a king deserving royal treatment. This victorious Christ best expressed the church's theological understanding of the crucifixion itself as the enthronement of God's Son.

"Vexilla Regis," written by Venantius Fortunatus, was first sung in 569 in honor of a relic of the true cross and is strikingly Johannine.[7] Sung during the offertory procession on Good Friday, it expresses the mystery that in the death of this body comes the life of the world. Here is no suffering Jesus. The only attack is the spear wound which inflicts no pain but instead insures sacramental life (Jn 19:34):

> . . . criminum
> Ut nos lavaret sordibus,
> Manavit unda, et sanguine. (lines 6–8)

Johannine paradoxes are stressed: life endures death; by death life is obtained; and, most succinctly, *Regnavit a ligno Deus* (line 12).

The cross is the standard of a king, *vexilla regis*. As in the proper preface for Lent, the tree becomes the symbol of both life and death. In this hymn the bloody tree becomes the royal throne, *ornata regis purpura* (line 14). In fact, the tree itself bears the pains of Christ, not only since it bears his body, but also because it assumes some of the pain which would be inappro-

7. Venantius Fortunatus, "Vexilla Regis," *The Hymns of the Breviary and Missal* 123–126.

priate for a victorious king. More than depicting a dying victim, Fortunatus describes a reigning monarch.

A superb elaboration on Fortunatus' metaphoric use of the cross is found in the Anglo-Saxon poem "The Dream of the Rood."[8] The anonymous poem has an obscure history, but the first and better half seems to date from about 700. Here John's technique of paradox is further developed. The cross is the "sige-beam" (victory-tree), both a gem-studded processional cross and the bloody place of execution:

. . . hwilum hit waes mit waetam bestemed,
beswyled mit swates gange, hwilum mid since gegyrwed.
   (lines 22–23)

(. . . sometimes it was soaked with sweat,
drenched with flowing blood, sometimes with treasure adorned.)

The cross assumes all the pains of Jesus: "purhdrifan hi me mid deorcan naeglum, on me syndon pa dolg gesiene" (Then through me they drove the dark nails, on me were the wounds seen) (line 46). The cross must restrain itself from falling down upon the enemies to crush them, for here the Johannine Christ does not even contemplate a release from death.

Christ is called *Weald* (Ruler), *Haelend* (Healer), *Frean* (Lord), and *Dryhtne* (Master). He is the archetypal Anglo-Saxon warrior of courage. In a language in which the noun for "male" is the same as the noun for "warrior," Jesus is "pa geong haelep, paet waes God aelmihtig, strang and stipmod" (that young hero, that was God almighty, strong and resolute) (lines 39–40).

Anglo-Saxon literature preserves tales of two chieftains, Beowulf and Byrhtnoth, famous for their courage, and this same "much courage," *elne micle*, is given both to the cross and to Christ. Not only does Christ go bravely toward death, but he "embraces" the tree of the cross. At the end Christ is not pitifully dead, but rather: "And he hinepaer hwile reste, mepe aefterpam miclan gewinne" (and he then there awhile rested, weary after that great battle-strife) (lines 64–65). The poem continually

8. "The Dream of the Rood," *Sweet's Anglo-Saxon Reader*, ed. Dorothy Whitelock (Oxford: Clarendon Press, 1967) 153–157.

stresses that the blood of the cross is the glory of life—very Johannine indeed!

The Good Friday liturgy of the Roman Church is Johannine in its development of Passover imagery, as the readings of Exodus 12, Psalm 22, and John 18 and 19 testify. The poem used during the veneration of the cross, the Reproaches, was compiled over the ninth through the eleventh centuries.[9] The speaker is the crucified Christ, who is the holy, mighty, and immortal God. The references to Isaiah 5 link the bitter wine of the unfaithful vineyard with both the wine Jesus drank on the cross and the sacramental blood from his side. The Reproaches recall John's portrait of Jesus who confronts his opposition: *Responde mihi* (answer me).

The details of the passion come from several gospel narratives: the lance is from John, the reed from Mark, the gall and vinegar from Matthew. Yet the thesis is Johannine, that the salvation of the Passover is mirrored in the details of the crucifixion:

I opened the sea before you,
and you have opened my side with a lance.
. . . .
I gave you the water of salvation to drink from the rock, and you have given me gall and vinegar to drink.

The great power by which God raises the chosen people is also the power on the cross. Although the Reproaches delineate all the sufferings of the passion, Jesus is anything but a helpless victim. He is, rather, a mighty God who has saved the people throughout history and who confronts them with mighty power.

A sixteenth century English lyric, "Tomorrow will be my dancing day," is popular still today.[10] The practice of rewriting a secular love song into a Christian carol was common in medieval times, especially in the cult of the Virgin. But in this carol the

9. "Good Friday," *The Liber usualis*, ed. Benedictines of Solesmes (Tournai, Belgium: Desclee, 1956) 720–751, and "Good Friday," *The Book of Catholic Worship* (Washington, D.C.: The Liturgical Conference, 1966) 93–99.

10. "Tomorrow will be my dancing day," *The Oxford Book of Carols*, ed. Percy Dearmer, R. Vaughan Williams, and Martin Shaw (London: Oxford, 1964) 158–159.

lovers are Christ and the church, and the incarnation, death, and resurrection of Christ are seen as gifts presented to the lover.

The carol's narration of the life of Christ stresses Johannine themes: the incarnation in "fleshly substance," the rejection by the Jews who "loved darkness rather than light" (stanza 6, Jn 3:19), and the spear wound which "issued forth both water and blood" (stanza 9). While several of the scenes are synoptic, the tone of confidence and joy is Johannine. Christ's ultimate power is acclaimed in the refrain, that everything occurred "to call my true love to my dance." Even in the sentence of death Pilate "judged me to die to lead the dance" (stanza 8). The meditation on suffering is replaced with the expectation of Christ's general dance.

Isaac Watts used this same technique of paradox in his excellent hymn of 1707, "When I Survey the Wondrous Cross."[11] The portrait is Johannine: Jesus is the "young Prince of Glory" (line 2) whose blood is a royal robe, his thorns a rich crown, his mien a grand nobility, the cross wondrous. The royal imagery is carried through into the last stanza, in which the poet offers all the world to his king of amazing and divine love. The hymn writer's incorporation of Pauline theology heightens the paradox of this triumphant king.

One must not imagine that the writers of these eleven passion pieces consciously selected one gospel over the others as their biblical inspiration. Indeed, through much of this period Mark was virtually unknown, and many people, then as now, knew the passion narratives mainly through gospel harmonizations. But it is good to realize that our passion plays, poems, hymns, and prayers do convey a certain portrait of the dying Christ, and thus a certain Christology. Is Jesus the abused victim? The loving savior? Or already on the cross the triumphant king?

This selection of literary pieces suggests that the stronger the image—a royal throne, a processional cross, the Passover, the general dance—the more powerful the depiction of the passion. John's Jesus is supreme not only within his gospel but through-

11. Isaac Watts, "When I Survey the Wondrous Cross." *The Handbook to the Lutheran Hymnal* 138–139.

out the tradition. This Jesus evokes not our pity but our adoration. It may prove instructive to test our own participation in the passion for the dominant images of Jesus and the Christology contained therein.

2

"The Dream of the Rood": A Translation

THE DREAM OF THE ROOD IS A POEM ABOUT A VISION OF THE TRUE cross. It was written by an unknown poet or poets about the eighth century in England. The poet uses a contemporary literary convention—the epic tale of the heroic warrior—to depict Christ, who, like Beowulf, is a victorious chieftain. In the poet's vision, the cross is intermittently both a glittering processional cross and the bloody cross of Calvary. As the cross tells the story, the cross itself bears much of the pain of the crucifixion, while the strong Johannine Christ, a true Anglo-Saxon warrior, is eager for the fray, weary after battle, yet completely triumphant. The poem commemorates the discovery of the true cross, and is therefore appropriate for use in the liturgy on Holy Cross Day, perhaps as a communion song, and during Holy Week.

The only extant manuscript of *The Dream of the Rood* is tenth century, but parts of the poem were engraved in runes on the eighth century Ruthwell Cross in Scotland. The poem is written in Anglo-Saxon, the language of England before the Norman Conquest, an inflected languge that is as close to modern German as it is to modern English. Anglo-Saxon poetry did not rhyme, nor did it have regular meter. Rather, it was held together by alliterative patterns. According to the rule, the first and/or the second foot (an accented syllable) alliterated with the third foot, but never with the fourth foot in each line. The rhythmic pattern is similar to that of the Gelineau psalms. Although the number of stresses per line is fixed, there can be many or few syllables in a line. Many sentences ended not at the end of a line, but at the midway caesura. Scholars believe that the poetry was chanted or declaimed by a scop (the poet or bard), while a stringed instrument marked the four stresses per line.

The poem has 156 lines, but many scholars believe that the second half, which is sermonic rather than imagistic, may be the work of a second writer. This translation is of the first 77 lines. I have sought to translate the poem quite literally, using cognates whenever possible and recalling the alliterative patterns of the original, while keeping the lines accessible to the ear for liturgical use.

The performance of the poem has been done quite simply: the chords for either guitar or piano and the chanting pitches provide a possible equivalent to Anglo-Saxon usage:

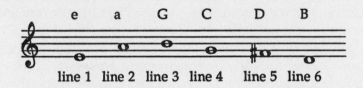

Circumstances will dictate whether the mood should be meditative or declamatory. If meditative, the singer will chant quite slowly with ample pauses. Only two strikings of the chord per line are appropriate to this reflective mood. The text is marked to indicate the first and third stresses in each line. If, however, the mood is declamatory, the voice will convey great excitement, and as many as four strikings of the chord are possible.

The singer changes pitch at the first stress of the line. The single tone per line can be simply embellished. Since this section of the poem is only a fragment, the poem ends with line 5 of the six-line musical pattern. To give a sense of conclusion to the performance, however, the musical accompaniment will finish the chord sequence, striking chords 6 and 1.

The following is an example of how these suggestions could be realized:

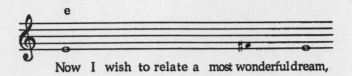

Now I wish to relate a most wonderful dream,

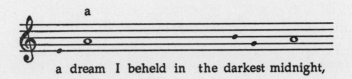

a dream I beheld in the darkest midnight,

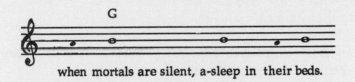

when mortals are silent, a-sleep in their beds.

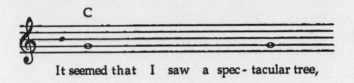

It seemed that I saw a spec - tacular tree,

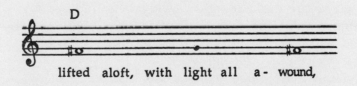

lifted aloft, with light all a - wound,

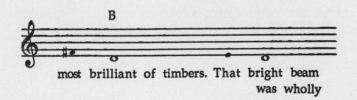

most brilliant of timbers. That bright beam
was wholly

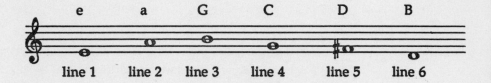

Now I wish to relate   a most wonderful dream,
a dream I beheld   in the darkest midnight,
when mortals are silent,   asleep in their beds.
It seemed that I saw   a spectacular tree,
lifted aloft,   with light all a-wound,
most brilliant of timbers.   That bright beam was wholly
gilded with gold.   Gems shimmered
beautiful at its foot,   and five there were
up on its arms.   Angel hosts gazed on it,
fashioned fair since creation.   That was no felon's gallows,
there beheld   by holy spirits,
by many on earth and   the whole mighty creation.
Marvelous was the triumphant tree,   but I stained with sin,
wounded with wrongdoing.   The wondrous tree I saw,
bedecked with banners,   brilliantly shining,
emblazoned with gold.   Jewels of great splendor
had covered with treasure   the tree of the Lord.
But yet through the gold   I glimpsed the strife
which was suffered so long ago,   for suddenly the right side
began to bleed.   Heartbroken, distressed,
I feared before that fair sight.   A transfigured beam,
it changed color and dress: now drenched with sweat,
bathed with blood,   but now beauteous with jewels.
And so there I lay   a long while,
sorrowfully beholding   our Savior's tree,
until it started   to speak. I heard
these words spoken   by that spellbinding tree:
"I remember it yet,   it was years ago,
I was laid low,   hewn down from the woodland,
felled from my stem.   Fierce foes seized me,
forced me to display   their felon to the skies.
Borne on warriors' shoulders,   I was set on a hill
and fixed there by foes.   I then saw humanity's Lord

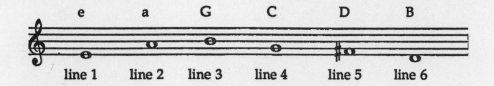

hásten boldhearted   to ascend upon me.
I did not then dare   against the decree of the Lord
to bénd or to break,   though I behéld trembling
the surface of the earth.   Súrely I was able
to féll those foes;   yet I stood fast.
The young hero stripped himself;   this was God almighty,
strong and stouthearted.   He ascended the hated gallows,
dáuntless in the sight of many,   to redéem humankind.
I trembled as the warrior embraced me.   I dared not bów to the
    earth;
I must stand fast,   not fáll to the ground.
I was ráised up a cross;   the mighty kíng I lifted high:
it was forbídden that I fall down   befóre heaven's Lord.
Dárk nails were driven through me,   déep wounds were seen,
gáshes made by malice.   Yet I must give no harm.
They derided us together.   I was drenched with the blood
that rán from his side   when he reléased his spirit.
There, on that mountain,   much I endured,
wicked events.   I watched the God of hosts
futhlessly racked.   Clouds of darkness
served as a shroud   for the corpse of the Lord.
Shadows overcame   the shining light
which was veíled under clouds.   All creation wept,
bewailing the king's fall,   Christ on the cross.
Then lóyal, ready,   they arrived from afar
to the side of the prince.   All this I beheld.
Laden sorely with sorrow   I bówed to human hands,
húmbly, boldhearted.   They laid hóld of almighty God,
lífting him from his great torment.   Léft there by the warriors,
I was washed with blood,   all wounded with barbs.
His limbs spent, they laid him down.   They stood by his head
and behéld there the Lord of heaven.   And he rested there
    awhile,

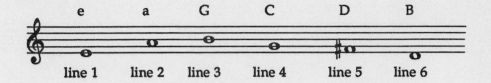

weary from the battle.   Warriors búilt him an earthhome
near the śite of the slaughter;   from bright śtone it was hewn.
There they láid their victorious Ruler.   The láment they chanted,
those ẃretched ones that evening.   Then ẃeary they traveled
aẃay from their triumphant Lord.   With a small tŕoop he rested
    there.
Yet ẃe were there grieving   a ǵood while,
śtanding on that site.   The śounds of the mourners
and śoldiers were fading.   His fĺesh grew cold,
that fáirest of lives.   Someone félled us at last,
áll to the earth: an appálling fate!
We were búried in a pit,   but the compánions of the Lord
unéarthed and upraised me;   the Rúler's thanes
adórned me, dressing me   in sílver and gold. . . ."

3

The White Hotel and the Feast of the Holy Innocents

LET US CONSIDER SOMETHING SELDOM PONDERED BY MOST OF US: THE slaughter of the innocents.

I recently visited the town of Siena in Italy. In my view its worst feature is the Siena cathedral. Indeed, one reason to visit the cathedral is to get a sense of how brutal and wretched European life was in the Middle Ages. For at the cathedral one still sees the construction site stopped midway. The walls were meant to double the Duomo's size, but then the Black Plague struck and Siena was decimated. The walls stand there abandoned, a mammoth tombstone to the thousands killed by the plague. Inside the cathedral are more signs of death, great mosaic floor tiles depicting Old Testament battles—though of course the soldiers' dress and weapons are period to the cathedral itself. It looks as if the part of the Bible which was known best was its warfare. And there, nearby the pulpit, is a scene in floor tiles, perhaps twenty by thirty feet in size, a depiction of the slaughter of the innocents. Herod is enthroned, ordering a dozen medieval soldiers to their task; fifteen women wail, contorted in their sorrow, already twelve babies lie dead under the soldiers' feet, and several more are being tossed on swords' edge, being eternally killed there on the floor tile of the Siena cathedral.

Why? Why would people dedicate in their church such a grotesque depiction of such a wretched story? And of course the Siena floor tile is not the only piece of medieval art in which the children are being slaughtered. In the Cloisters in New York City

23

there is a set of wood panels, carvings from a fourteenth century abbey church—perhaps the wainscotting in the choir—and there too is a slaughter of the innocents: two cruel soldiers' faces, the baby dead in the air. Not only art, but also poetry seemed intrigued by this story. In a poem from the Byzantine liturgy, the number of dead infants has escalated to 14,000, the grim tale growing in horror. *The Oxford Book of Carols* boasts seven carols specific to this day.

Let us recall the story, told by Matthew (2:16–18):

Then Herod, when he saw that he had been tricked by the magi, was in a furious rage, and he sent and killed all the male children in Bethlehem and in all that region who were two years or under, according to the time which he had ascertained from the magi. Then was fulfilled what was spoken by the prophet Jeremiah:
"A voice was heard in Ramah,
wailing and loud lamentation,
Rachel weeping for her children;
she refused to be consoled,
because they were no more."

On these few verses rests the grotesque art which leaves us wondering. However, these verses give us not only a history of art, but also a continuing liturgical observance on December 28. In the year 1997 December 28 will fall on a Sunday, and the lessons of the slaughter of the innocents will be read throughout Christendom. Choirs will sing the Coventry Carol, of "Herod the King in his raging." So close upon our cultural oogling over the infant in the manger comes this story of screaming infants and wailing parents. We call these children martyrs, those killed for the sake of Christ. We dress in red, not for bows and Christmas berries, but for flowing blood, and remember the death of the infants near to the life of the newborn Jesus.

Why? Why the Siena floor tile? Why this observance and its proximity to Christmas? Ought we celebrate such brutality? How can we make a festival out of the murder of children? How can we commemorate the slaughter with Christmas trees still up?

There is the question of historical accuracy. Some biblical interpreters provide ample discussion of the difficulties in this story and make us question whether it even ever happened.

How can we jive Luke's history with Matthew's? What is our continuing debt to old stories we no longer wish to believe? Even Raymond E. Brown, in his massive study *The Birth of the Messiah*,[1] who tries valiantly to give the story both historical credulity and religious meaning, admits that in Bethlehem and its environs there were at most twenty boy children, twenty at very most.

Let us leave this question for a few moments to talk about a novel by D.M. Thomas entitled *The White Hotel*.[2] D.M. Thomas, a little known British poet, published a novel which both as hardback and paperback was a bestseller for months. The reading public devoured the book, and the literary critics as well raved about the quality of the writing. The novel is about a twentieth century woman named Elizabeth Erdman who in 1919 sought psychiatric assistance from Sigmund Freud to deal with her severe neurotic symptoms. The book begins with records of her wild sexual fantasies, but always her ecstasy is held parallel to the horrendous suffering of those around her. We then read Freud's diagnosis. Not surprisingly, he analyzes her neurosis as related to her parents' sexual problems, but even he admits that his theory cannot probe the deepest level of Elizabeth's suffering.

The novel goes on. In 1929 Elizabeth, much improved, meets and marries an older Jewish man. She has a new light on her past, for, devout Catholic that she is, she suspects that she is really half Jewish. Her suffering is then placed in the broader context of global anti-Semitism. But she becomes a loyal wife and mother in the Jewish quarter of Kiev.

But the novel goes on. Kiev in the 1930s was no place for a Jew to live. Elizabeth finally joins the rest of Kiev's Jews, herded towards the ravine, machine-gunned into a mass grave at Babi Yar. She could have saved herself, with that crucifix around her neck, but she chose to stand by her Jewish stepson. She dies at Babi Yar, reciting the Ave Maria.

But the novel does not conclude with the Nazi soldier raping this old woman with a bayonet. There is a final chapter: wonder of wonders! The Jews really did take the train to Palestine! Elizabeth and all of Europe's Jews are in a refugee-camp-styled Par-

1. Raymond E. Brown, *The Birth of the Messiah* (Garden City, New York: Doubleday, 1977).
2. D.M. Thomas, *The White Hotel* (New York: Viking, 1981).

adise, where spayed cats give birth, but where human beings still bear their earthly wounds.

This novel is a picture of this century: our obsession with the meaning of sex; our focus on the individual neurotic; our interest in cultural roots; our struggle with family systems; our history of anti-Semitism; our recognition of global evil; the fact of genocide; our partial images of the resurrection. This book of death and life is well worth reading.

This novel talks about the world. The truth of this novel describes individual, familial, social, and global agony. Our word "agony" comes from the Greek word *agon*, meaning struggle. No matter how effectively Elizabeth can conquer one struggle, another harder one is forthcoming. We too turn from private pain only to encounter familial and social and global agony.

The question for the liturgy is how to offer that pain to God. How can we make the liturgy open to such pain as Elizabeth knew? In past decades we tried by writing new liturgies filled with versicles about Viet Nam and responses about world hunger. Most of these liturgies are now lost in file cabinets, for the language we wrote was simply not accurate enough, not deep enough to bear the weight, not open enough to individual suffering. We wrote labored confessions of sins in which we confessed everything from nuclear stockpiling to migrant worker oppression. We prayed intercessions in which we told both God and the people in the pew how to solve all the problems of the world. It was not wrong so to do. But it fell short.

We need not compose labored "liturgies." In the classic liturgy of the western church the words about the terror of our hearts in this age surround the word, which is Christ. It is not that the liturgy bears the world on its shoulders, but that Christ does, and has, and will. There on the deepest level of our liturgy is Christ, bonded to the agony of human life. Let us look at several familiar parts of our liturgy, examining their images, to find the Word of God amid the words of our troubled life.

"The sign of the cross may be made." So we begin. This is no petty gesture, placing ourselves under the sign of Christ's cross, donning that death, recalling that living water. It is a more radical gesture than kneeling, which all religions prescribe; more surprising than the kiss of peace, a cultural tradition turned Christian. No. The sign of the cross is an act of faith in the horror and the glory of Christ's cross. The cross says both holocaust and paradise. It says, in this sign I conquer: I die in the water and rise to dance. This is no small thing. It is Christ dying and alive, the word in the world.

We sing the Gloria, an exuberant hymn of praise. But here too the song hears the wretched cry of the world. The call of the angels, "Glory to God!", greets the shepherds, the poor of an oppressed land, begging for a Messiah. Some lines further we sing another Kyrie: Lamb of God, slain for our safety, your blood on our door, have mercy on us. We are only lowly petitioners before the divine throne. We then call Christ the "Holy One." Remember who also did that? The demoniac, the madman looked at Jesus and named him the Holy One of God. So in the Gloria we keep motley company: magnificent angels, grubby shepherds, terrified Hebrews, lowly petitioners, screaming wildmen. With them all we praise Christ, the word of God alive in such a world as this, for such people as this.

Then there are the intercessory prayers. It seems that if we really believed in the efficacy of prayer, we would spend a good deal longer praying. And we need not feel required to tell God the way to solve the world's problems. We need only to hold up before God the wretched of the world and to plead for God's grace. We can be far more inclusive than we usually are. D.M. Thomas' novel would remind us to pray for tormented and lonely people; for wretched family situations; for ghetto people and for refugees; for those who are persecuted; for those who today will die. Look on them, O God, with tearful eyes, and grant your grace to all.

We come then to the eucharistic prayer. Many contemporary Christians pray the Hippolytus prayer, written in the second century. "He is your Word," we pray with the ancient Hippolytus. It is he, we acclaim, who in order to destroy death, to break the bonds of the evil one, to crush hell underfoot, to give light to the righteous, taking bread and giving thanks, said, Take and eat. Note this grand sentence: Christ said take and eat, and so destroyed death and crushed hell. The life of eating and the death of Christ are held together, even in one sentence, the bread of life shared in the face of death.

Finally let us return to our beginning, to the festival of the holy innocents. Here is the birth of God next to the slaughter of the Bethlehem children. Christmas is, after all, not about Santa Claus, but about God's hearing the cries of wailing Rachel, God's hearing that cry in Christ. "Rejoice insofar as you share Christ's suffering," says the second lesson for the day, as the death of the toddlers, and our death, shares in the death of Christ.

Let us hear the Episcopal and Lutheran prayer of the day:

> We remember today, O God, the slaughter of the holy innocents of Bethlehem by order of King Herod. Receive, we pray, into the arms of your mercy all innocent victims, and by your great might frustrate the designs of evil tyrants and establish your rule of justice, peace, and love, through your Son, Jesus Christ our Lord.

There is a lot in this prayer: we recall a holy story; we plead for God's mercy on all who suffer; we plead for God's might to bring on the kingdom. Those words contain the woes of countless human predicaments. We remember the infant boys killed by the Pharaoh of old. We know that Herod ordered his soldiers to murder various prominent citizens at the moment of his death so that there would be grief in the land. There was Mary, holding her dead son. Thousands died with bullets in their back at Babi Yar, and today innocents are being slaughtered in Iraq and Lebanon. For all these we plead mercy. We know the injustice and hate and war which describe the human race: against all this we plead God's might.

Much of the language of the liturgy is like this: it is metaphor. Metaphor is both simpler and deeper than descriptive and analytical language. It says less and covers more. It offers an image, a picture, a story into which we exert ourselves, our praises and our pleas. One could call the liturgy a corporate recital of images of the faith in praise of God. We assemble under the cross. We sing with the angels, at the Exodus, in God's throne room, with the demoniac. We are the soldiers and the wailing women, we are even the dead babies. We use these images to say that we are the world, and we hold these images up to Christ for rebirth, for new life from the Word to this world. The Word speaks in the world because, while the baby Jesus escaped death this time, a later Herod condemned him to a death for us.

And so while I would vote against a grotesque floor tile in any church depicting bleeding babies, I admit that such an image has more to do with the Christian faith than many of our sappy pictures of Jesus or, worse yet, our ignorant pictures of God. Our God, says Hebrews, is a consuming fire; therefore we are to worship God with reverence and awe. The human need to hold together life and death in God: the liturgy can help us to this endeavor, the liturgy with its texts, its lessons, its festivals.

4

Children's Literature for the Religious Imagination

THANKS TO THE MINISTRATIONS OF A DEVOTED AUNT AND A FAITHFUL friend, my daughters have been graced at Christmas and birthdays with an astonishing collection of children's books. Although not released by church publishing houses, many of these books are religious in content or theme, and because of their excellence in text and art should be more widely known in church circles. This review will cover a dozen of my favorite picture books for the preschool child with the hope that parents, religious educators, and clergy will find ways to use such superior religious literature in the shaping of their children's Christian education. With my imprimatur comes my confidence that merely the eloquent reading of such books as these could become the focus of nursery and elementary church school and thus serve as the primary complement to the children's worship in the regular Sunday assembly.

Noah's Ark, illustrated by Peter Spier (Garden City, New York: Doubleday and Company, 1977) is a picture book of remarkable detail depicting the story of the flood. The opening drawing of a victorious army leaving a burning city as Noah tends his vineyard sets the context for God's call of Noah, as well as providing occasion for conversation about human warfare and the eucharistic wine of God's peace. The pictures are delightfully comic—the elephant stepping on a mouse's tail—and realistically poignant—the water rising up the legs of all the animals who did not get elected to enter the ark. The picture of the rising sun and the olive branch in the dove's beak is one of the better depictions of the Trinity we could show our children. In the end Noah is again planting a vineyard, readying the children for the eucharist after the flood of their baptism.

Despite all the storybooks of Christmas published by religious publishing houses, it was at the check-out counter of the grocery store that I found the Little Golden Book's *The Animals' Christmas Eve*, by Gale Wiersum, illustrated by Jim Robison (Racine, Wisconsin: Golden Press, 1977). In simple iambic stanzas the barnyard animals, first one, then two, up to twelve, tell the story of the incarnation. Not only the Lukan details are told, but also the Christian meaning of the story: "Ten soft lambs say Jesus' name. / 'He was the lamb of God who came.' " The book is able to narrate both the story and its meaning for the church—an uncommon feature among the countless Christmas books on the market.

Perhaps the most astonishing Christmas storybook available is Barbara Helen Berger's *The Donkey's Dream* (New York: Philomel Books, 1985). The donkey "with a load on his back" carries Mary to Bethlehem, dreaming that on his back is a city, a ship, a fountain, and a rose. When the child is born and the man shows the donkey "what we have carried all this way," the donkey sees in the newborn child the city, the ship, the fountain, and the rose. The illustrations in this book of fantasy are powerfully imaginative and provide a splendid primer for typology, for without didactic explanation the book works within the imagination to merge the great metaphors with the pregnant Virgin and so with Christ. I was quite blown away.

The True Cross by Brian Wildsmith (New York: Oxford University Press, 1977) merges Bible story with legend in a book of spectacular illustrations. Wildsmith relates the medieval legend that it was a sprig from the Tree of Life in the Garden of Eden which grows into a miraculous life-giving tree and eventually is used for the wood of Jesus' cross. The tale of St. Helena's discovery of the true cross concludes the book. The legend has important religious value far beyond any question of its historicity, for the legend superimposes in our religious imagination the verdant Tree of Life with the dread tree of the cross. I came to the Tree of Life only as an adult, and am grateful to this revival of the medieval legend so that my daughters see in the cross "a magnificent tree," with birds finding "shelter among its enormous branches."

Several other fine books are based on medieval saints' legends. *Saint George and the Dragon*, adapted by Margaret Hodges, illustrated by Trina Schart Hyman (Boston: Little Brown, and Company, 1984) is a beautiful book with formal illustrated margins and full-page pictures of the adventures of St. George and his terrible fight with the dragon.The Red Cross Knight bears the sign of Christ and vanquishes evil for Una, who can be seen as the needy, or the Virgin Mary, or the church. The story is open to many levels of interpretation, as readers of Edmund Spenser's *Faerie Queene* are aware; yet for the preschool child we have a lively and lovely tale of the power of sacrificial service for the good of the other.

Another such medieval legend in a version with enduring power is *The Clown of God*, told and illustrated by Tomie dePaola (New York: Harcourt Brace Jovanovich, 1978). This French tale of the old beggar who juggles before the statue of the Madonna and Child will give our children so much: images of medieval life, the memory of the circus, care for the beggars they see, acquaintance with two periods of artistic depictions of the Mother and Child, knowledge of the symbol of the orb. But mostly the book gives a moving example of God's acceptance of our gifts and God's transformation of our simple golden balls into liturgical signs of divine life. I am delighted that it is during the liturgy that old Giovanni gets the idea to juggle for the Child in the Lady's arms. *The Clown of God* is recommended also as a book dealing with death, for the old juggler dies, simply and sadly, when performing for the Christ child.

Also by Tomie dePaola is *The Legend of the Bluebonnet* (New York: G.P. Putnam's Sons, 1983). Here a Comanche Indian legend tells how a little girl's love for her people inspires her to sacrifice her precious doll to the Great Spirits, in hope that they will send rain. The next morning the mountain of her sacrifice is covered with the bluebonnet flower, and the rains begin. Her name is changed, from She-Who-Is-Alone to One-Who-Dearly-Loved-Her-People. The Indian girl is an image for us not only for our own Christian lives but also for Christ himself. At a time when there are still too few feminine images for God available to our children, this tale of the sacrificing girl is a superb addition to your library.

The Miracle Child, told by Elizabeth Laird, with Abba Aregawi Wolde Gabriel (New York: Holt, Rinehart and Winston, 1985) tells another story of a child miraculously providing food for his people. This Ethiopian tale of St. Tekla Haymanot uses illustrations from an eighteenth century mánuscript of this thirteenth century folk hero. The fantastic miracles ascribed to St. Tekla Haymanot provide a context for older children (ages 7–10) to probe the role of faith assertions in religious self-understanding. Of course, ten-year-olds do not use adults' sophisticated categories in their search for the truth of faith: they use such books as *The Miracle Child* as imaginative ladders for their climb.

It seems to me that the major point of children's catechetical instruction is to educate children in their participation in the liturgy. Thus I am interested in books which purport to be guides through the liturgy. Most are terrible, because they are didactic and dull with mindless literalistic pictures of uninspiring liturgical action. But there is Graham Oakley's *The Church Mouse* (New York: Atheneum, 1972), in which the mice take boat rides in the font, Sampson the cat falls asleep during the parson's sermon and a riot ensues, and the animals know the robber "must be a terrible chap because he hadn't bothered to take his hat off in church." Such a delightful story taking place in the church and during the liturgy is a fine addition to your library.

The Boy Who Could Sing Pictures, written and illustrated by Seymour Leichman (New York: Holt, Rinehart and Winston, 1973) ought to be on seminary reading lists in liturgy courses, but before such an enlightened day it can at least be on your shelves. Ben, the court jester's son, discovers his miraculous ability to sing pictures. When he looks out at the poor peasant audience, he sees "the great sadness. It hung in the air. It curled like a snake in the chimney smoke. This sadness was a living thing and it was his enemy." So he sings about doves and the river and the rainbow, and the people see the joy. "No one cheered. You do not cheer a miracle." The illustrations of his songs are, my daughter reminded me, like Chagall's paintings. But when Ben must sing before the wicked, cruel king, his song is different. The rhetoric of this amazing book echoes the Book of Revelation, overflowing with superimposed, bizarre images of life and death. May it be that our liturgies, like Ben's song, sing the Promised Land.

In the religious formation of our children, we must regard their dreams—daydreams, night dreams, nightmares—as imaginative recreations of life and death, of the children's trying on their lives in a new way. Such dreams are the ingredients of saints' legends, of the Book of Revelation, of the images of baptism and the eucharist. Two fine and quite opposite books on dreams I would add to your list. Maurice Sendak's famous *Where the Wild Things Are* (New York: Harper & Row, 1963) turns a boy's rebellion into an adventure in which he conquers rebellious creatures, and in taming the monsters, tames himself. He returns to his room, the forest gone, "where he found his supper waiting for him, and it was still hot." May it be that our little Maxes, having tamed their monsters in their boat ride over the ocean, are welcomed to the table.

When Everyone Was Fast Asleep, by Tomie dePaola (New York: Puffin Books, 1979) takes two children on night adventure of meeting the elf horse and dancing at the palace, of visiting the trolls, "but we were not afraid." The Fog Maiden leads the children through the fantastic dream, a gentle dream of peace and possibilities. If *Where the Wild Things Are* can be the dream of drowning the demons in baptism, *When Everyone Was Fast Asleep* is an image for slumber in God's Dream Maiden, a rest in rich images of joy and communion. Instead of silly exercises of asking children to draw heaven, I would read to them of the Fog Maiden.

The truth is that many supposedly secular books are essentially religious by being about God, the human search for the divine, the quest for truth, the need for human communion. Children's books, following the tradition of illuminated manuscripts, juxtapose text to image and in a remarkable way evoke primordial images of death and life and enliven our religious imagination. Probably because of budget restrictions, possibly because of editorial trepidation, religious publishing houses print denominationally safe children's literature. It goes almost without saying that such work cannot be profoundly about God, for images of God are not safe. Rather than a stupid picture of God as a crowned old man, here we have seen God as the Fog Maiden, Christ as an Indian girl, the liturgy as Ben's song, the Christian life as St. George's battle against the dragon, the incarnation as a fountain on a donkey's back. These books are mainly for preschoolers: we must not waste these years. All too soon my daughters came home with Beverly Cleary and Judy Blume, realistic comic light fiction about girls getting through the day. As I believe that what will really get my children through their day, through their life, is a repository of images of life in death, I am grateful to such authors as these for the foundational images these splendid children's books can give.

SUBMITTING TO SYMBOL

5

Mary as the Symbol of Grace

CHRISTIANITY IS A RELIGION IN WHICH ONE IS USUALLY SAYING SEVeral things at the same time. There are those words like "kingdom" or "bread" which have several different meanings and varied usages, and nearly anything you choose to speak of— take, for example, baptism—has any number of metaphoric names. Sometimes this multivalence of Christian religious language leads to explicit paradox: that is, language means the exact opposite of what it appears to mean. In the finest Christian religious language, words mean both what they appear to mean and the direct opposite. St. John's Gospel teaches us to use words in this way. "To lift up" means, for John, both for Christ to rise to the Father and for Christ to hang on the cross. Indeed, Christianity says that in paradox is the truth: Christ goes to the Father by being hanged on the cross. Neither is true without the other. The words mean two things at once, simultaneous opposites, and within the tension is the truth.

Christian liturgy is filled with examples of such multivalent language. In the "Holy Holy Holy" we sing two ancient songs: the sacred hymn of the angels surrounding the heavenly throne of God, and the boisterous chant of the Jerusalem folk surrounding Jesus on a donkey. We surround the table of bread and wine, and we quote the angels and the Jews in order to say: Isaiah's God and Israel's Jesus are one in the same, here praised in this bread. Even our language *about* the liturgy is multivalent. Is that piece of furniture an altar or a table? To be either Christian altar or Christian table, the piece of furniture must be both, and whatever word we use must contain the paradox of Christian worship: offering to God and sharing a meal.

Yes, but. Yes, A means B, but it also means C. Yes, A means C, but it also means Z.

Most of us today are scientists; we want A to equal B, simply and easily, without any "Yes, but." Excelling in physics is more acceptable socially than excelling in poetry. Metaphoric language, in which words have several meanings at once, is always difficult to sustain.

One can see our slipping away from such multivalence by examining our use of the term "grace." Some people use the word only to signify table prayer. In my tradition, "grace" is used as a synonym for Christ's death on Calvary. God's grace equals forgiveness which comes through Christ. In other traditions one sees this usage of "grace" in the phrase "Have you got grace?", which could be translated "Have you appropriated to yourself Christ's crucifixion?" or "Have you accepted Christ's forgiveness?" In this usage, grace has one level, for forgiveness is as great for the infant as for the murderer. In this usage, grace always comes down, from God to humankind, in the cross.

However, like other multivalent Christian concepts, grace is not so easily defined. It is not a simple, one-directional action. Grace denotes communication, relationship, and life together. An expression like "growth in grace" tries to say that while grace is Christ's gift from Calvary, it is also a continuous way of life in which one can participate. "Tom is a grace to me," I might say, meaning that through Tom I receive some of the life of God. "Grace" is a way of naming the life of union between God and God's baptized people: God with them, they with God, and they with one another.

Since most of us are neither systematic theologians nor linguistic philosophers who like to wade through such complicated language, religion uses symbols which encapsulate the multivalence of truth. Our task is to keep alive the multivalence of the Christian symbols. This constant task is required on all levels at all times. From the toddler afraid of the dark, to the theologian who knows it all, the gospel calls out "Yes, but."

There are many ways to talk about Mary. Countless historical, theological, and devotional studies concerning this central woman abound in human history. However, let us focus on one small aspect of Mary: Mary as the model of the paradox of grace—multivalent Mary.

Often, Mary is dealt with as the maid of Nazareth. Mary is meek. She is minding her own business when out of the blue she is called by God. She claims nothing for herself, not even her own humility, but obediently hears and bears the Word of God. My own teachers interpreted the scarcity of New Testament texts concerning her life to mean that she remained a humble, even an insignificant person. While our clergy would have marked "true" to the examination question "Was Mary the Mother of God?" they surely never called her by that title. Mary is the maid of Nazareth, standing wholly dependent on the grace of God, and as such is a model for humankind.

In some traditions of piety, Mary is divine. As Queen of Heaven she rules with God, granting favors and dispensing grace of her own power and by her own right. Fully graced by God, she is now entirely of God; she is Queen as God is King.

No matter which extreme has been our respite from the tension of truth, our knowledge of religious truth will pull us back into the paradox. Mary is both the maid of Nazareth and the Queen of Heaven. She is the humble girl, but also the mother of God. She is the image of the church, but she is a Jewish woman. We, who have been baptized in that womb-tomb and nourished by that bread-body at that altar-table, can grow to be comfortable within the tension of paradox: "maid-Queen" is the truth. The ancient councils knew this in their Christological term, Virgin Mother of God. Can a virgin be a mother? Can God have a mother? Christian truth grows within the cracks between human language.

The metaphoric names for Mary point to this paradox. The Fathers enjoyed the image of the New Eve and spun out all the ways in which Mary is and is not Eve. Mary is the Daughter of Zion, the Bride of Christ, and the Mother of the Church, all at once. Mary, as the dwelling of God, is a metaphoric goldmine: the pregnant woman, the ark of God, and the church itself are all dwellings of God. (And, of course, this is the incarnation: that this pregnant woman is the ark of God.) Grace visited Mary with the divine without removing her from the human, and that miracle is the Christian mystery.

It is a cheap shot to point both to excesses in Marian devotion and to total disregard for Mary. One of the church's tasks in this ecumenical time is to find ways to venerate Mary so that she remains both maid and Queen. If she is only a maid, the implications of her connection with Christ have not been considered. If she is solely a Queen, the depths of the incarnation have not been fathomed.

A theory of symbol can help explain this. Mary is not a sign which, like a wedding ring, conveys information. That is, "Mary" is not merely the name of Jesus' mother, a historical personage whom we can either recognize or ignore. Nor is Mary a signal, a presence triggering our genuflection, an automatic indication of certain expressions of piety. She functions for the church rather as a symbol—a living reality which grows with our participation in it, which embraces us in relationship, which includes us in its mystery. Always that mystery in which she includes us is the mystery of Christ. With her we enter Christ, as Christ enters her and us. And, as Christian mystery, she is always "Yes, but." Yes, hers is the white veil, but hers is also the jeweled crown.

One way in which to see the papal promulgations of Marian doctrine is to recognize which specific human conditions the church has addressed in the doctrine. Our talk of Mary and our interpretation of her as receiver and participant in grace is a prelude to talk of ourselves as graced ones. Mary is maid and Queen, and we are sinners and saints. The more we allow Mary to contain the paradox of grace, the more we might be able to fathom that paradox for ourselves and to join her in that life of God. It is easier to play the role of sinner or to glory in our sanctity than it is to live within the paradox of sinners and saints.

In the multivalence of religious language we say that Mary is the mother of the church, bearing Christ in the world, standing at the foot of the cross, the first to live anew in the kingdom of God. Yet calling Mary Mother ought not to keep us from calling also God "our Mother," God who bears her people in pain and who nurses them with her own body. Mary as maid and Queen, God as Mother and Father: it is all feeble human language (graced as much as it is able) to talk about God, and thus brings us to the divine by bringing the divine to us.

Mary, *maid of Nazareth, you show us the life of humility.*
Mary, *Queen of Heaven, you shine before us in the light of Christ.*
Mary, *Virgin Mother, you are given to us, a mystery of God.*
Mary, *Mother of God, teach us your magnificat: for God has looked with favor on me, a lowly serving maid; from this day all generations will call me blessed.*

6

On Meeting Mother Rome

MY FATHER'S NAME IS MARTIN LUTHER. MY HOME HAS BEEN ON THE whole a good one, but all the rooms, excepting the kitchen, have always been crowded with men: Adam, Jeremiah, Paul, Luther, Melanchthon, doktorvaters and pastor-fathers, friends who are men who became pastors, and pastors who are men who became friends, all drinking German beer and preaching loud sermons. But it is as if I found the family tree, hidden in a basket in the attic. There! There is my mother's name: "Go ye forth to meet her." So I climbed down several flights of stairs to explore among the foundations, and quite a trip to Rome it was.

On the worst afternoon, the kind that hits all tourists in Rome eventually—it was St. Rita's Day, St. Rita of Impossible Cases— we couldn't locate the lost raincoat because we couldn't make a phone call because we didn't have a telephone token because whenever we bought candy or wretched Italian gum, the vendor gave us change in tiny bills or none at all, and the banks naturally were *chiuso*-ed. There alongside our frustration was an outrageous Baroque church, inside cool and dim, and at a side chapel was Bernini's statue of the ecstasy of St. Theresa. And so in the midst of no telephone tokens, I lit a candle by St. Theresa and prayed for my ex-Mormon colleague back home.

An aged nun, bent back, bent neck, full black habit on a hot May day, rutted face, four feet tall, unlocked for us the ruin which is St. Stephens in the Round. She was not smiling beatifically, as Mother Teresa always is.

Down in the catacombs a marble stone marks the place of the bones of a five-year-old girl. The inscription is simple: a bird, two ChiRhos, words stating her name and age.

Up the sacred steps I went, up (they say) with Jesus, blood staining the marble, Pilate at the head. St. Helena brought them here to Rome from Jerusalem, they say. I do not know about Helena and Jesus, but I know that the bandana-bound woman next to me and countless other faithful, and Martin Luther as well, went up these holy stairs on kneeling knees.

On the hill where there was once a temple to the mother goddess stands St. Mary Major, the mammoth holy court of our Queen; the gilded ceiling and gilded arch and gilded apse and majestic columns draw your eyes to adore the Lady, the tiles' golden pattern swirls you forward to holiness. This throne room, nearly empty of objects, is pregnant with a stunning presence. The walls must be thick, to keep so much splendor inside and off the streets of Rome. Meanwhile, in the little neighborhood church across the Tiber, in the old Jewish quarter named Trastevere, in the mosaic of the apse, Christ is crowning Mary. She sits, somewhat aslant, at his side, the panoply of stones, with gold and silver, clothing the Queen in a robe which shimmers more than real brocade, more than the solid gold mantle covering our Lord.

But if I had to tell you only one story from Rome, it is of San Clemente I would speak, for there beyond all else I met Rome. She was, to begin with, in the twelfth-century church with its inlaid paschal candlestand and its third reading desk, built solely for the chanting of the Exultet. She was in the profuse mosaic of the tree of life which graces the apse. She was also in the lower church, the fourth century basilica, dug out with spoons last century by obedient Irish Dominicans. She was in the frescos fading fast from those newly-exposed walls, the picture of Mary as if she were an empress at court, pearls in her hair, and the painting of the woman converted by St. Clement whose husband was not a bit amused. But there is more: for Rome is also in the layer below this ancient church, where is an apartment house in which old Clement may actually have lived—although I did not find her in the Mithraen school and temple, all those men drinking too much wine and eating symbolic bull. Rome here at San Clemente was finally in the onrush of clear water, water pure to drink, gushing under this deep ground—at one corner you can reach down to spray up the surging water. I have never heard such loud water, flooding the silence of this ancient relic, drowning out our silly games, we pretending to be Clement's family discussing the Mithraists across the street. The water flows through a Roman aquaduct, built here, only two blocks away from the Coliseum, to carry water to the games for sea battles or to wash blood away from the gladiator frays, who knows. The womb of water underlies it all: Clement, the bull, the alleyway, the hidden church, the praying Dominicans, the tree of life, the tourists, the postcard shop.

I met more of my mother in two Florentine annunciations. At the Uffizi gallery was a fourteenth-century Martini painting, the angel's words printed on the gold background, the Virgin drawing away from the greeting, her shoulder protecting her breast as a woman's body retreats from too intense a lover. At San Marco the Dominican novices walking up the stairs to their single cells would have been greeted by Fra Angelico's annunciation, a pure radiant Mary, an angel in woman's appearance, a small gold design on the angel's gown, the word proclaimed, utterly silent. And although also in Rome there were gypsy children dirty for begging, the gypsy whom I cannot forget was in Florence: a woman younger than I, garishly dressed, her head swaying in a loud incoherent and fragmented chant, her blouse open and her empty breast pacifying a daughter who looked perhaps four years old, emaciated and with eyes more vacant than the mother's.

From Siena I will try to forget the dried-up head of St. Catherine, cut off I believe in St. Raymond's final unconscious oneupsmanship on the woman who had so commanded his life. From Siena I will try to forget the mosaic tile on the cathedral floor: who could have judged it a good idea to consecrate a nearly life-sized depiction of the slaughter of the innocents, all those women wailing for the dozen dead babies under the soldiers' feet? From Siena I will try to remember the early painting of Catherine, a woman younger than I, writing books and lecturing clergy and praying urgently to God.

At Assisi I saw my emptiest room, the barren dormitory in which Poor Clare met Sister Death. At Assisi I had one of my happiest surprises: entombed nearby to Francis, in that solid austere crypt are not only his first four companions, but also "Brother" Jacoba, the Roman woman whom Francis loved and who loved Francis. "Ama, ama, ama" was embroidered on her trousseau veil which covered his face for burial.

In Ravenna I diminutive stood before all those mosaics, ornate brocaded robes on all those holy women, as if the multicolor stones were planted and blooming alive like tulips in Holland, as if the gilt were sun's rays over a lake. The Empress Theodora and her court are offering a jeweled chalice of wine; the procession of saints is beautiful in magnificent gowns, presenting gifts to the Virgin and Child. But the mosaics, grand as they are, are not as grand to me as the fact that the holy women are there, even numbers with the men, able to offer. I went back several times to the tomb of Galla Placidia—did she design it?—circles of stars on the entrance vault, the rainbow of remarkably contemporary geometric designs bordering the scenes, the mosaics changing in color as the sunlight moved through Ravenna's sky that day.

And through it all, cats! I had not known that there was a cat at the Last Supper, but in a Uffizi tapestry, and in a Florence fresco, and in a Siena window, a cat is rather too near Judas. And I recall the nursing cats and balls of kits nesting like their generations before them in the ruins of the Roman forum.

I could go on. Of course there was more. Some night it will be other images shaping my dreams, another day perhaps masculine memories. But I judge that I have indeed met my mother. Now I must decide with whom to live, with her or with my dad.

7

Typology as Biblical Symbol

IN THE NINETEENTH CENTURY HYMN BY JOHN JULIAN, "O GOD OF GOD, O Light of Light," is the following quatrain:

> Deep in the prophets' sacred page,
> Grand in the poets' winged word,
> Slowly in type from age to age
> Nations beheld their coming Lord.[1]

Probably many twentieth century Christians, upon singing the line "Slowly in type from age to age," see in their imagination—as I did when a child—thousands of books, type on the page, libraries full of type, marching on down to Bethlehem. This meaning of the word "type" is understandable in our print-oriented culture. But the pity is that a prior meaning of "type" has been lost. For were healthy typological interpretation of the Scriptures reborn among us, much good would come our way, especially in the three areas of homiletics, catechesis, and liturgical art. By typology I mean a Christological interpretation of the Hebrew Scriptures in which Old Testament persons, events, and symbols stand as types or images of Christ, the church, and the sacramental life.

The contemporary church is bereft by its abandonment of typological thought. Although typological interpretation was com-

1. *The Lutheran Hymnal* (St. Louis: Concordia Publishing House, 1941) #132.

49

mon in the early church and although liturgical art utilized typology for 1500 years, a number of tendencies have worked against an acceptance of typology and have conspired nearly to eliminate its use altogether. There was the historicizing mentality of the fourth century of which all readers of Egeria's journal are aware. The desire in the empire church to locate the holy sites and to keep vigil on the exact anniversaries led the church away from interpreting Easter as passover and towards understanding Easter as the memorial of historical events in Jesus' life. The nineteenth century belief that history could tell the literal truth encouraged the practice of approaching the Hebrew Scriptures as the chronicles of the ancient near eastern ancestors of Jesus of Nazareth. For biblically oriented denominations, this meant children memorizing the kings of Judah and the kings of Israel, without any imaginative connection made between these kings and Christ the King.

The move of seminaries to approach the Scriptures in solely an historical-critical frame of mind further accentuated this problematic tendency. Several years of intensive biblical study leave seminary graduates attempting to date individual passages and to judge the historical accuracy of the accounts. Surely much good has come from the historical-critical method, particularly in the church's ability to understand more deeply the meaning of any biblical passage in its own milieu, the better to make the transference necessary into the contemporary situation. But the method has also deprived many clergy of the liturgically important skill of interpreting images. As one pastor said, "Now that we know the angels were invented by Babylonian art, why should we sing the Sanctus?" But history is not only about accuracy of record: indeed, revisionist historians, pointing to the subjectivity of writers, remind us how little facticity such records can have. However, history gives images for contemporary identity, and a certain telling of history shapes present meaning by providing the very categories in which the human narrative is framed. Such a reading of the Bible as images overflowing with meaning is too often neglected in contemporary seminary education.[2]

2. Gordon W. Lathrop, "A Rebirth of Images: On the Use of the Bible in Liturgy," *Worship* 58 (July 1984) 292–97.

The tendency in western art in this millenium toward realism also worked against typological interpretation. Instead of depicting Christ as a youthful shepherd or baptism as Jonah's adventures in the sea, the Renaissance gave us the unsettling combination of Jesus in the first century with Jesus in the Renaissance, so that Michelangelo's Last Judgment has as much to do with the artist's interior struggle as to do with a portrait of Jesus. The eastern icon tradition has tried to resist this tendency. But when we read the pronouncement of the Great Moscow Council of 1665—"To represent the God of Sabaoth (that is, the Father) on icons with a gray beard, with his only Son on his lap, and a dove between them, is exceedingly absurd and unseemly"[3]—we realize that even iconographers were forgetting the merits of the typological depictions of God as the three visitors to Abraham. Radical Protestant iconoclasm did its share of damage, and a century of fundamentalism also militated against imaginative biblical imagery in the churches.

The Enlightenment conception of language, evident in the average preacher's assumption that words have a single undisputed meaning, has worked against a healthy typological use of words. A scientific frame of mind has suggested that words, like mathematical symbols, are objective signs for specific exterior reality. Such a search for single reference clarity has been devastating to poetic modes of perception, in which the multivalent character of acquired and accumulated meaning is revered as the better means towards truth. In *The Great Code* Northrop Frye suggests that the west's fascination with scientific definition has reached its limit.[4] We are witnessing a return to metaphoric meaning and mythic forms in many places; there is still time to reject the notion that a rock is a large stone and no more and to return to the imaginative exercise of wondering what all that rock might be.

More contemporary phenomena could be cited. Since the Holocaust many Christians have feared that typology necessarily leads to anti-Semitism. Thus they have argued against such

3. Leonid Ouspensky and Vladimir Lossky, *The Meaning of Icons*, trans. G.E.H. Palmer and E. Kadloubovsky (Crestwood, New York: St. Vladimir's Seminary Press, 1982) 204.

4. Northrop Frye, *The Great Code* (New York: Harcourt Brace Jovanovich, 1982) 12–15.

Christological interpretation of the Hebrew Scriptures. But we shall see that anti-Semitism can be avoided and need not, even when coinciding with historical scholarship, realistic art, and linguistic analysis, finally bury the skill of typological interpretation. Yet one more difficulty in our time with typology is current biblical illiteracy. Old Testament references are lost on a people who have never learned the biblical narratives and ancient images. In the toy department of Macy's department store, the clerk did not know what a Noah's ark set was, and in a college philosophy class only one student, a conservative Jew, knew who David and Bathsheba were. But lest we become discouraged by the present situation, let us look for inspiration to a remarkable exercise in typology which the thirteenth century has bequeathed us, typological studies called *Bibles Moralisées*.

During the thirteenth century a number of typological "Bibles" appeared. These picture books were comprised of several thousand pairs of roundels: the first medallion of each set depicted the biblical scene in narrative order, and the second showed its meaning for the sacramental life or moral decision. Several Latin copies of the *Bible Moralisée* are extant.[5] References in this paper are to a French translation of the *Bible Moralisée*, an incomplete manuscript with about 1000 roundels covering Genesis through 2 Kings.[6] While the Old Testament text covers the stories chronologically as if it were primarily historical narrative, the purpose of the *Bible Moralisée* is to teach the typological significance of the Old Testament images. The Old Testament event is respected, but a Christological meaning is unfolded. A brief accompanying text in the margin explains the intricacies of the comparison. The *Bible Moralisée* is not a laborious allegory, as we might expect from the medieval mind, but instead displays a more primitive patristic exposition of images characterized by ingenuity rather than consistency. In its linking of Old Testament images with the New Testament and the sacramental life, the *Bible Moralisée* suggests to us possibilities for homiletics, cate-

5. *La Bible Moralisée*, Illustrée, Reproduction Intégrale du Manuscrit du XIIIᵉ Siecle, 4 vol. (Paris: Société Française de Reproductions de Manuscrits et Peintures, 1911–21).

6. *Bible Moralisée*, Faksimile-Ausgabe im Originalformat des Codex Vindobonesis 2554 der Österreichischen Nationalbibliothek, Reihe Codices Selecti Vol. XL (Graz: Akademische Druck-u. Verlagsanstalt, 1973).

chesis, and liturgical art, as well as warning us of the danger of anti-Semitism.

THE OLD TESTAMENT AND THE LIFE OF CHRIST

As we might expect, many of the Old Testament roundels in the French *Bible Moralisée* are paired with scenes from the life of Christ. A familiar example is the depiction of Isaac carrying the wood towards the fire while Abraham watches, paired with Jesus carrying his cross toward Golgotha while thirteenth century Jews watch. The typology is evident already in the Isaac picture, for the wood he carries is in the shape of a cross. Such Christological comparisons abound. Noah lies naked before his sons, while Christ stands naked on the cross. In most of the Joseph cycle, Joseph is a type of Christ. Joseph's dream shows Joseph acclaimed by his brothers, while Christ is worshiped by the disciples. Joseph's brothers show Reuben that Joseph is not in the pit, while the angels show the women that Christ is not in the tomb. Jacob is shown his son's bloody cloak, while the holy women see the bleeding Christ. An official brings Joseph up out of prison and a servant clothes him, while God raises Jesus from the grave and an angel clothes him. Other major characters are also types of Christ. The Egyptian princess finds Moses lying in the basket, while Mary, as the New Testament church, finds Christ lying in the great pulpit Bible. David slays Goliath with his sling and staff, while Christ slays the devil with the gospel book and his cross. Nathan sits Solomon on a mule to acclaim him king, while Christ enters Jerusalem on Palm Sunday.

This pattern of Christological interpretation follows New Testament practice. In Romans 5 Paul explicates the story of Adam's fall for its Christological meaning. In Acts 8 Philip explains the gospel to the Ethiopian beginning with an interpretation of Isaiah 53. The early Christians continued to read the Hebrew Scriptures because therein they encountered the gospel. All our essential Christian vocabulary—LORD, Christ, sacrifice, word, lamb—comes from the Old Testament. The New Testament is a Christian gloss on the language and the imagery of the Old Testament; it is as if the baptized believers are saying, "When we say lamb, we mean Christ." The paschal sermons of the first several centuries are filled with this reliance of the New on the Old Testament. We read in the second century Easter homily of the Melito of Sardis:

> Therefore if you wish to see the mystery of the Lord,
> look at Abel who is similarly murdered,
>   at Isaac who is similarly bound,
>   at Joseph who is similarly sold,
>   at Moses who is similarly exposed,
>   at David who is similarly persecuted,
>   at the prophets who similarly suffer for the sake of Christ.
> Look also at the sheep which is slain in the land of Egypt,
>   which struck Egypt
>   and saved Israel by its blood.[7]

Ambrose, Augustine, and Gregory of Nazianzus continue this tradition. Martin Luther, in his prefaces to the books of the Bible, judges which Old Testament books are most valuable for the church because in them Christ is most clearly proclaimed. For Luther Christ is more clearly evident in the Psalms than in the New Testament book of James: thus the church should use the Psalms more than James in public worship.

Perhaps nowhere do we see this redefinition of Hebraic images by the Christian gospel more clearly than in the title Lord. We ought to be sympathetic to current unease with this term because of its masculine overtones. Yet if we substitute another word, it must be a term which replaces YHWH, translates both the Hebrew title *Adonai* and the Greek title *Kyrios*, and is synonymous with emperor: perhaps Lord is the best option. This single word demonstrates the Christian demand for typology: for the holy name of God, the Almighty of the Hebrew Scriptures, is now granted to Jesus of Nazareth.

Such typology which illuminates the Old Testament with the light of Christ would have a great effect on contemporary liturgical preaching. Many churches have now recovered regular reading of the Old Testament lessons and recitation of full psalms. But as the recovery occurs, the church must be clear about its purpose. We do not read the Old Testament narratives

7. Melito of Sardis, *On Pascha and Fragments*, ed. Stuart George Hall (Oxford: Clarendon Press, 1979) 33.

to increase our knowledge of ancient near eastern history, to be enlightened by old myths, or to be inspired by Hebrew poetry. Christians read the Old Testament in the eucharistic assembly because therein they see the gospel. The psalms as well, although they can be read as poems about a self-reflective consciousness, function far better in public worship if they are keyed to Christology and their meaning linked to us through baptism.

Christian reading of the Old Testament has long sought to tie Old Testament images with their antitypes in the New Testament. However, negative reaction to the unfortunate Roman habit of reading only snippets of the Old Testament has led to an alternative plan, the lectionary of the Consultation on Common Texts, in which there is sequential reading of Old Testament stories. It would be better to improve the typological choice and to lengthen the selections than to adopt the CCT plan. The main difference between the two lectionaries is that in the summer months the CCT lectionary offers continuous readings of the Old Testament narratives: cycle A the stories of the patriarchs and matriarchs, cycle B the kings, cycle C the prophets. It is argued that in this way the Old Testament is read "in its own right" and that such consecutive reading of the narratives will educate the people in Bible history. Whether parts of stories read seven days apart in the middle of summer will teach the assembly the Bible is hard to say: but the church must always beware of turning the liturgy into Bible history or catechesis. Furthermore, eliminating the link between the first and third lessons produces three stray lessons and makes even less likely the ideal of a liturgical homily which comments on the links made by the three lessons. However, the first claim—the hope to encounter the Old Testament as Old Testament—is the one which we must address here.

The liturgy need not be overly concerned about encountering "the real Old Testament." The Hebrew Scriptures are read in the Christian assembly because in them we are given an old language of faith transfigured in Christ. We do not read the tree of life vision of Ezekiel 17 as yet another example of tree of life images in world religions. Christians read about Ezekiel's vision because that great mythic tree, giving nest to birds of every sort, stands in radical contrast to the mustard "tree" of Mark 4, which is no great tree at all, but a slight bush, paradoxically becoming

a sign of the mysterious dominion of God in Christ. The attrac-
tiveness of the Old Testament narratives may accentuate the
problem in that there may be an increase of Old Testament topical
preaching with little or no reference to the breaking of these
stories over the cross. The narrative of Elijah and the still small
voice in 1 Kings 19 should not be turned into a pep talk about
courage: instead Christians see it paired to Jesus' stilling of the
tempest in Matthew 14, Christ himself the still small voice, the
word of God crucified for us. The continuous readings of the
Old Testament as suggested in the CCT lectionary, rather than
encouraging Christian knowledge of the Old Testament, will
undermine the main reason that Christians read the Hebrew
Scriptures in their assembly.

One defense of the CCT's proposal to read the Old Testament
narratives argues for the moral lessons such stories teach. But
let us look at one of the Old Testament's most famous tales of
intrigue, the love story of David and Bathsheba. I ask you: what
is the moral lesson of David and Bathsheba? That murderers and
adulterers are punished, or at least scolded? Many biblical rogues
were not. That adulterers will be blessed with a Solomon? Of
course not. In fact, David is not reprimanded for extramarital
sex: in accord with the code of his time, Nathan's parable con-
demns David for having stolen Bathsheba who was the property
of another man. I suggest that the moral of David and Bathsheba
is the same found in Jesus' rescue of the adulterous woman: that
God is merciful towards human nature. Any attempt to gain
contemporary ethics from the Old Testament must jump several
hurdles along the way: the vast differences between the cultures
and Paul's challenge in Galatians 3–5 for a new Christian ethic.
It is interesting that in the French *Bible Moralisée* David and Bathsheba are seen as types of Christ and Lady Church, their union
being the sign of God's grace.

THE OLD TESTAMENT AND THE SACRAMENTAL LIFE

About one third of the roundels in the French *Bible Moralisée*
link Old Testament images to the sacramental life. Already on
the first page, God draws Eve out of the side of Adam, while
God draws the church—a figure holding a chalice—out of the

side of the crucified Christ. Much of the Moses cycle is cued to the sacramental life. Moses removes his shoes before the burning bush, while Christians remove their clothes before God for baptism. God gives Moses his staff, while God gives the church Christ. The Israelites mark their homes with a tau, while Christians mark their Romanesque church, complete with chalice, with a crucifix. The menorah is likened to the seven doves, gifts of the Spirit. We realize that communion was in decline and that already three hundred years before the Reformation, the word was central, when we see that Old Testament images of eating, like the Israelites capturing the quail from God, are likened not to the eucharist but to Christians hearing the word. The water taken from the rock is likened to the book taken from the altar. The spies carry back from Canaan a great bunch of grapes, while bishops and monks carry a crucifix in procession. Communion is implied only rarely: Abimelech gives David and his hungry band the holy bread of the presence, while a priest communes believers with the bread, round cakes marked with a cross. A picture illustrating the description of the temple in Leviticus is likened to a twelve-arched Romanesque church, the arches filled with the faithful. A procession around Jericho with the ark of the covenant is likened to a procession with the reserved sacrament.

We could multiply examples. But let us go back instead, to 1 Peter 3:21–21, where Noah's ark is likened to baptism, to see that such typological connections between the Old Testament and the liturgical life were common in the tradition. Particularly the mystagogical catechesis of the third and fourth centuries is filled with such connections. Tertullian likens the primeval waters at creation and the bitter waters made miraculously sweet to the water of baptism. In an Epiphany sermon Gregory of Nyssa said:

> Even before the incarnation of our Lord, the ancient Scripture everywhere prefigured the likeness of our regeneration; not clearly manifesting its form, but foreshadowing, in dark sayings, the love of God to man.[8]

8. Gregory of Nyssa, "On the Baptism of Christ," *A Select Library of Nicene and Post-Nicene Fathers*, 2nd series, ed. Philip Schaff and Henry Wace, Vol. V (Grand Rapids: Wm. B. Eerdmans, 1979) 541.

Gregory lists as types of baptism the water Hagar receives in the desert, the well by which Isaac's servant meets Rebekah, the wells Isaac dug in the desert, the well by which Jacob meets Rachel, the water in which Moses was hid, the crossing of the Jordan River by Joshua, the water used for the sacrifice of Elijah on Mt. Carmel, and the river water by which Naaman is cured of leprosy, as well as the water mentioned in the poems of the psalms and prophets. With lively enough imagination, nearly any amount of water can be seen as a type of baptism, and all God's feedings as types of the eucharist.

One of the finest examples in contemporary liturgy of this typological connection between Old Testament images and the sacramental life is the Exultet. In this ancient hymn of the Easter proclamation, Easter night is likened to the day of Christ's atonement, the paschal feast, the crossing of the Red Sea, the darkness of sin, the chains of death, and hell itself. The single paschal candle shining in the dark church is described as if it were the creation of light at the beginning of time, the splendor of God's radiance, the blood over the doorposts, the resurrection of Christ, and Christ as the morning star. This great poem proclaiming the resurrection does not mention the cross, the three days in the tomb, or the characters of the passion. The figures attending our liturgical celebration are typological: Adam, the children of Israel, the bees who made the candlewax. In the same way as the Exultet, the lessons of the Easter vigil rely on typology to speak liturgically. We await the resurrection not by grieving with the disciples but by rehearsing the ancient types of baptism and the eucharist: the creation of the world from primeval waters; Noah's salvation through the flood; Abraham's sacrifice of the ram; the crossing of the Red Sea; Isaiah's call to the feast on the mountain; the life the Spirit gives to the valley of the dry bones; the passover; even the three men in the fiery furnace, in which God enters the place of death with the faithful so that they emerge victorious. Unless we revive typological interpretation our attempts to reinstate the Easter vigil as the preeminent Christian celebration will be thwarted by lack of understanding.

Our efforts at catechesis would be greatly assisted by our relearning the typological use of the Old Testament images in expounding the liturgical life. In many of our churches mystagogy, the catechesis of the baptized towards a richer sacramental life, is in miserable disrepair. The Roman phenomenon of the Rite of Christian Initiation of Adults is one attempt to deal with the problem. But the majority of Christians still are baptized as infants, and as they grow, the efforts to teach them the Bible and the meaning of the sacraments are meager indeed. As a child I learned the Bible, though not the sacraments: that was at least something. Too often, in challenging the historicity of the flood, we do not teach it any longer. A lively option would be to teach it better than before, not as a past historical event occurring to others, but as a type of the baptism which transfigures us today. The same is true for expounding the eucharist. We can do little to reinstate the mythic family meal, the better to teach the meaning of the eucharist. Yet even if our culture still enjoyed daily elegant and hospitable family dinners, instead of cold pizza on the run, the Old Testament stories would still be central to our understanding. For it is God with whom we dine, we, like Moses and the elders in Exodus 24, eating and drinking with God on the mountain. It is far more useful for children to link manna with the communion bread which, it is devoutly to be desired, they share, than it is for them to speculate on the accuracy of the account, or what is increasingly the case, never to have heard of manna at all. From age three upwards the stories can be enthusiastically received as images of the child's baptism and weekly communion. Sooner or later, of course, the child will ask how Moses' staff got water out of the rock. But several years before, the child can see that the rock, like the baptismal font, flows with living water for all when touched by the wood of the cross.

THE OLD TESTAMENT AND LITURGICAL ART

In the increasingly problematic area of liturgical art we look to the *Bible Moralisée* for both what and what not to do. The *Bible Moralisée* exemplifies the kind of liturgical art used most extensively in the western church. The drawings on the walls of a family burial room in the catacomb of St. Sebastian in Rome depict the entire narrative of Jonah as the way to affirm Christian faith in resurrection through baptism. Jonah's story is surely a better way to depict the resurrection than the ridiculous pictures which were part of my catechesis of fully clothed people half out of their graves rocketing up into the sky. How can liturgical art draw a picture of the church? The *Bible Moralisée*, in offering a contemporary parallel to the Exodus narration of the building of the tabernacle, shows a Romanesque church building in which Mary is holding in her hands the reigning Christ, Peter is holding the keys, Paul is holding a sword, and a martyr is holding his scalp. Compare this with many contemporary pictures of the church: photographs of the exterior of a church edifice.

Many churches are cleaning house these decades, discarding great piles of junk which passed as liturgical art and designing liturgical space with an almost Puritan sensibility. Presiders no longer have an embroidered head of Christ on the rear of their chasuble upon which to sit, and garish paint is removed from saccharine saints to reveal the stunningly simple wood underneath. But little by little liturgical art is reentering the churches, as money becomes available for a new altar frontal or a fine processional cross. Yet contemporary western art is highly individualistic in its expression. Whether the art is abstract or representational, traditional symbols are debunked in an idiosyncratic search for meaning. Thus it is unlikely that art shaped by these contemporary trends will be able to serve the liturgy. Perhaps granting current privatized connotations of the word art, we must think not of church art but of liturgical craft.

Perhaps were liturgical artists to bone up on the Scriptures, they would have the raw materials for depicting life in the church. As a thirteenth century English monk wrote, in defense of typological art in the church:

Since the eyes of our contemporaries are apt to be caught by a pleasure which is not only vain, but often profane, and since I did not think it would be easy to do away altogether with the meaningless paintings in Churches, especially those in Cathedrals and Baptisteries, where people congregate in large numbers, I have thought it an excuseable indulgence that they should be attracted by that class of pictures which, as being the books of the laity, might suggest divine things to the unlearned, and stir up the learned to the love of the Scriptures . . . Therefore it is, that in order to curb the licence of painters, or rather to influence their work in churches where paintings are permitted, my pen has drawn up certain applications of events in the Old and New Testaments, with the addition in each case of a distich which shortly explains the Old Testament subject, and suitably applies the New Testament one.[9]

We need to recall San Vitale in Ravenna with its typological mosaics flanking the altar: Abraham's hospitality to the three visitors and Abraham's sacrifice of Isaac. Marc Chagall's painting "The White Crucifixion," with its scene of pogroms, burning synagogues, and at the bottom of the canvas, the Jewish mother shielding her infant, has as its central image Christ on the cross: his loin cloth is a prayer shawl. There is Chagall's "Exodus," in which the crowd of Jews has crossed the Red Sea (is it fire, or blood?); Moses holds the tables of the law; and above the refugees, Christ is crucified. More homespun artists than Chagall are able in new ways to cast the biblical images with reference to Christ. Brother Eric de Saussure, a member of the Taizé community, uses a neo-icon style in his work. His rendition of the sacrifice of Isaac shows a calm Abraham and Isaac walking arm in arm, and behind them a third man, carrying the wood. ("Who is the third who walks always beside you?" writes T. S. Eliot in *The Waste Land*.[10]) Perhaps in this time of returning biblical illiteracy we again need liturgical art which like the Gothic stained glass window tells the biblical stories and which resembles those Orthodox icons into which we are physically inserted. If people will not read their Bibles at home, perhaps they will profit from looking at pictures in church. One obviously wasted medium is the bulletin cover. Often adorned with a drawing of the church building or a sentimental photograph of a sunset, this piece of paper could well depict the biblical scenes of the lessons, perhaps the Old Testament and the gospel, modeling itself exactly on the *Bible Moralisée*.

9. "Pictor in Carmine," quoted in M. R. James, "On Fine Art as Applied to the Illustration of the Bible in the Ninth and Five Following Centuries, exemplified chiefly by Cambridge Manuscripts," The Cambridge Antiquarian Society's Communications, Vol. VII (Cambridge: Deighton Bell and Company, 1891) 59–60.

10. T. S. Eliot, *The Waste Land*, in *The Complete Poems and Plays* (New York: Harcourt, Brace, and World, 1958) 48.

But in one respect we must reject the model of the *Bible Moralisée*. The thirteenth century manuscript makes no distinction between its depictions of God and of Christ. For several roundels in succession, perhaps, God is a bearded man wearing a blue starred cloak, and Christ an identical bearded man in a crimson cloak: but there is not much consistency here. In roundels in which God and Christ both figure, it is as if twins were depicted. Often the second roundel does not make clear whether God or Christ is intended. It was a mistake of enormous ramifications that religious art, even liturgical art, began drawing pictures of God. The Hebrew prescription against graven images is most profoundly not an outsider's condemnation of pagan religious devotion, but a believer's conviction that God is beyond both human imagination and artistic representation. Thus we reject even the most often reproduced picture in the *Bible Moralisée*, the full page frontispiece of God as a bearded man, bending over the work of creation, measuring out space with a thirteenth century compass.

THE PROBLEM OF ANTI-SEMITISM

It is not only the pictures of a masculine God which detract from the delights of the *Bible Moralisée*. There is an unrelenting anti-Semitism displayed in the typology. A great many of the six hundred sets of roundels in the French manuscript make an anti-Semitic comparison. Already in the sacrifices of Cain and Abel, the anti-type shows God accepting the bread of the Christian, likened to Abel, but rejecting the offerings of the Jew, likened to Cain. While Moses draws near to the burning bush, the Jews move away from the fire of God. King David gives to a servant the letter calling for Uriah's death, and the servant gives it to a soldier: God gives the tables of the law to a Jew who gives them to a devil. Solomon must choose between the two women, one with a live and one with a dead baby; God chooses between Lady Church, who is guarding a group of Christians, and Dame Jewess, who is guarding money bags. Dozens of the depictions of contemporary Jews show them clutching money bags. It would be tasteless to continue listing these sad examples of typology gone wrong, of the Hebrew Scriptures used to defame the Jews themselves. Because many people fear that such anti-Semitism must necessarily, or at least inevitably, follow from typological interpretation, they avoid the technique altogether.[11]

In anti-Semitic interpretation, a fulfillment theology has taken over with a vengeance. The Old Testament narrative becomes the "before" of the real story, seen in the New Testament. The contrast belittles the Hebrew story by making it a reverse image of Christ, a foil to truth. We children of the Holocaust must avoid the least suggestion that God's promises to Israel are laid aside or God's love for the Jews inadequate. But this distortion occurs only with typology gone wrong. In Romans 11, Paul likens Israel to a cultivated olive tree, living and growing by God's grace, into which Christians have been grafted. Christians do not cut down the olive tree, but grow into it, being able through Christ to tell its stories as their own. When the Exultet sings out that Easter is the night of the passover, the poem does not demean the passover or—as unfortunately the *Bible Moralisée* does—suggest the death of the Jews along with demons and sea monsters. Rather, the Exultet claims Passover as an image of salvation in Christ. The particular meaning of the old story is underlined by the way of the cross.

Great care must be taken to avoid anti-Semitism. Even Melito of Sardis began his homily with exhilarating poetic images of the passover, yet concluded by reviling the Jews. The difference lies in one's identification with the images. For example: if the story in Mark 5 of the hemorrhaging woman is taken as an image of suffering folk who reach out to us, woman has become a symbol of others' weakness. There is a difference, however, if the preacher identifies with the bleeding woman as an image of humanity, of us here, our life seeping out and we all reaching for Christ. To interpret Old Testament images as denigrating contemporary Jews is to forget Luther's cry that the Scriptures are *pro me*, for me, images with which I am to identify. Thus the offerings of Cain and Abel are about us: perhaps our attempt in whatever way we can to offer God praise; perhaps our religious ritual too distant from our interior state; perhaps our deepest doubts about the justice of God. Certainly we need not liken

11. See for example Gerard S. Sloyan, "The Lectionary as a Context for Interpretation," *Liturgy* 2 (1982) 43–49.

God's curse of Cain with a supposed rejection of the Jews, as the *Bible Moralisée* unfortunately does. Instead, the mark of Cain can be likened to the tau on our forehead at baptism, saving even such as us from the judgment we fear. In the *Bible Moralisée*, Naomi is accompanied by Ruth and abandoned by Orpah, while Lady Church is accompanied by Christians and abandoned by Jews. On the other hand, in the Lutheran lectionary, the story of Ruth is read as the first lesson on St. Mary Magdalene's Day, both women serving as images of the baptized who although surrounded by death return to the place of death, not even hoping to encounter God, but both discovering more of God's mercy than they had imagined, both becoming vehicles of God's grace to the world. That is a Christian interpretation of Ruth, sans anti-Semitism.

Some years ago the religion editor of the *New York Times* ran a front page story on Good Friday in which he quoted a prominent Jew's judgment that the Reproaches were anti-Semitic. Many Christians took the Jewish criticism to heart and discontinued use of this Good Friday ritual poem. Yet only a people bruised by centuries of anti-Semitic interpretation would construe this masterful poem of typology as offensive. Unfortunately, Christians' record in this matter being so abysmal, contemporary Jews do take offense at the Reproaches. But the Reproaches—"O my people, what have I done to you," Christ cries out to the church from the cross—are not inherently anti-Semitic. The Reproaches use Old Testament imagery to describe God's goodness to us and our rejection of that goodness through our sin. The people's response, far from any condemnation of first or twentieth century Jews, is a mantra-like plea for mercy: "Holy God, have mercy on us." The American Methodists have provided a version of the Reproaches which makes the charge of anti-Semitism impossible, for the typological use of the Old Testament images is carefully made explicit.[12] In fact, anti-Semitism becomes yet another example of crimes of "O my people," one of Christians' rejection of God's grace. Perhaps wider use of this version of the Reproaches would free us to resurrect this stunning poem of the passion and would educate the faithful in the gracious purpose of typology.

12. *From Ashes to Fire*, Supplemental Worship Resources 8 (Nashville: Abingdon Press, 1979) 156–59. Don Saliers, author.

The *Bible Moralisée* not only provides the lover of images several pleasant days of deciphering, but also gives substantive encouragement for our common tasks of preaching the lectionary, teaching the sacramental life, and adorning our liturgical space. The basic formula is simple: all of created life—not merely Old Testament persons and events, but also the natural things of the universe and the symbols of world religions—all things for the Christian come together in Christ. All things find their deepest meaning when mirroring the grace of God on the cross, by which their more particular meaning is not denied, but only expanded. Christian missionaries no longer destroy the culture they visit. A Lutheran pastor in Cameroon sees in the native Gbaya legends and rituals of the life-giving *sore* tree a type of Christ and so teaches Christ through the native symbol.[13] This missionary has opened the image up further and there discovered Christ. That is all typological interpretation is: the opening up of everything and there encountering Christ. For Christians there is one shepherd, but perhaps the other flocks have other images of Christ who is the image of God. Let us be about the labor of birthing again the old creative typology, for the deepening of our preaching, our catechesis, and our art, and for the happy surprise of finding images of grace where we had been too nearsighted to see them before.

13. Thomas G. Christensen, "The Gbaya Naming of Jesus" (Th.D. dissertation, Lutheran School of Theology at Chicago, 1984).

8

The Cross and St. Francis

"Above all the graces and gifts of the Holy Spirit which Christ gives to His friends is that of conquering oneself and willingly enduring sufferings, insults, humiliations, and hardships for the love of Christ. For we cannot glory in all those other marvelous gifts of God, as they are not ours but God's, as the Apostle says: 'What have you that you have not received?'

"But we can glory in the cross of tribulations and afflictions, because that is ours, and so the Apostle says: 'I will not glory save in the cross of our Lord Jesus Christ!' "

Little Flowers of St. Francis[1]

SERVANT OF THE CROSS

"WE CAN GLORY IN THE CROSS," SAID FRANCIS TO BROTHER LEO. SO Francis concluded his eloquent description of perfect joy. With the sign of the cross he summarized his inspiration for life, the sustenance of his vitality, the focus of his commitment.

Francis' subjection to the cross had begun long ago in the empty church of St. Damian when the lips of Christ, painted on

1. *Little Flowers*, 8, in *St. Francis of Assisi—Writings and Early Biographies: English Omnibus of the Sources for the Life of St. Francis*, edited by Marion A. Habig, 3rd revised edition (Franciscan Herald Press, 1973) 1320.

that cross, spoke to him about his mission. Francis had seen a vision of the living Christ; he heard the cross and obeyed. When he taught his companions how to pray, he advised them to offer first the Lord's Prayer and then this prayer of the cross: "We adore you, Lord Jesus Christ, here and in all your churches in the whole world, and we bless you, because by your holy cross you have redeemed the world."[2] The story tells that the Little Brothers reverenced every cross they passed, whether a jeweled crucifix in a sanctuary or a rude cross on a hillside. They should prostrate themselves, Francis urged, in devotion to the cross of Christ. He himself meditated on the cross, crying out over the love of God, mourning the wounds of Christ. When asked the reason for his constant lament, he answered, "I must weep for the passion of my Lord Jesus Christ; and I should not be ashamed to go weeping through the whole world for his sake."[3] For Francis, devotion to the cross was a sign of gratitude for Christ's passion.

Francis filled his letters with this sign of the cross. He reminded his readers about the passion; he reverenced the eucharistic bread as the body of Christ broken on the cross. He imagined the depth of divine love which poured out blood in death; he sought amendment of life as a response to the death of Christ. One of his letters, still extant and enshrined as a relic in Assisi, is signed both with Francis' own name, his signature, and also with the "tau," the signature of the Christian. Where Francis discovered the "tau" we do not know. Ezekiel first mentions it as the sign on the forehead of God's elect. It is the sacred mark of protection mentioned in the Book of Revelation, the sign of the cross which the church traces on the forehead of the faithful at their baptism and of the penitent on Ash Wednesday. This "T" mark, the "tau," merges with Francis own name, because he took the sign of the cross as the sign for himself.

THE STIGMATA OF CHRIST

Francis' devotion to Christ's cross occasioned the remarkable, mysterious experience which we call the stigmata. The Francis-

2. Francis, *Testament*, in *Omnibus* 67.
3. *Legend of the Three Companions*, 14, in *Omnibus* 901.

cans had been given a mountain in the Apennines by a friend of the Order. Francis used this desolate outcropping of rock as a place for religious retreat. He was praying alone there, fasting for forty days, in gratitude to St. Michael the Archangel. On September 14, 1224, the feast of the Holy Cross, Francis' companion called to him the opening lines of Morning Prayer. Francis did not return the expected response, and the Little Brother went to check on him. The brother found Francis, lying prostrate, still dazed by the vision of the Crucified which he had experienced.

The story tells that the vision was an Angel of the Lord, Christ as a seraph, the Crucified One in blinding light, his brilliant body held like a cross. The vision conveyed in terrifying splendor both the divine majesty and the human agony. In his religious ecstasy Francis experienced an identity with the Crucified which he later could not describe. He had so adored the Crucified One, he had so sought to imitate Christ, that he was marked with the cross of Christ and joined with Christ in praising God.

Francis spoke little about this experience in the few years remaining to him, but the sign of the cross was there. This was not only the "tau" sign cheerfully made, consciously drawn, as part of Francis' signature. Now he had other marks, deeper signs—the stigmata. After the experience of religious ecstasy, it became known that Francis' body bore the five wounds of Christ. Bonaventure writes:

> His hands and feet appeared pierced through the center with nails, the heads of which were in the palms of his hands and on the instep of each foot, while the points stuck out on the opposite side. The heads were black and round, but the points were long and bent back, as if they had been struck by a hammer; they rose above the surrounding flesh and stood out from it. His right side seemed as if it had been pierced with a lance and was marked with a livid scar which often bled, so that his habit and trousers were stained.[4]

Although Francis attempted to hide these bloody signs of his life with Christ, his closest companions caught sight of the wounds under wrap. The brothers who laundered his habit used

4. Bonaventure, *Major Life*, 13, 3, in *Omnibus* 731.

cold water to remove the blood stains. Not a beatific light emanating from his face, not the power of miracles, not a royal crown, but a bloody habit and wounded hands were his image of Christ. He wore his sleeves longer now, and put socks on his bare feet, as if these wounds were private, inexplicable signs of a visit from the Crucified.

Two years later, Francis died. Those who attended his body after his death were amazed by the wounds still present, still red with blood against the stark whiteness of the dead skin. On his body he bore the marks of Christ, they said, quoting Paul. They revered this simple singer of ballads, this disinherited bum, this itinerant preacher, as one uniquely associated with the suffering Christ.

One story goes further, recalling that at his death a flock of skylarks who gathered to praise or to mourn flew off to heaven in the shape of a cross, remembering in their reverence that sign which was both the impetus to Francis' vibrant vocation and the stigmata on his wracked and bleeding body.

THE WAY OF THE CROSS

Francis' sign was the cross. The Crucified One was both the model and the source of his life. To be like Christ, Francis embraced Lady Poverty. To follow the Christ proclaimed in the gospel, Francis heard and preached the word. He was devoted to the eucharist because he adored the Crucified One. He repaired churches because they were houses for the worship of Christ. He united with all creation to praise God because in Christ he saw the incarnation of God in all the created world. He effected reconciliation because as the companion of Christ he extended God's peace to all. He heard the Crucified speak because he identified with the sufferings of Christ. "In all things Christ," one could say of Francis.

Both his own Franciscan Order and Roman Catholicism in general have been nourished by Francis' vision of the Crucified One. Franciscan devotion to the cross led to the development of a pious exercise called the Way of the Cross. While stations of the cross were erected for devotional purposes in various places during the first Christian millennium, the practice blossomed especially when the Franciscans took charge of the holy places in Jerusalem following the crusades of the fourteenth century. Respect for the sites along the route of the crucifixion led to the practice of setting up models of the road to Calvary in parish yards and on monastery grounds. Usually there are fourteen stations, marked with shrines. The pious penitent travels the Via Dolorosa from the condemnation of Christ by Pilate to the burial of Jesus in the tomb. The faithful walk from one station to another, meditating on the passion of Christ, praying for amendment of life and for the coming of God's kingdom. Originally only Franciscan churches could possess stations of the cross. Today, virtually every Roman Catholic church in the world has on its walls or in its floors some representation of the way of the cross.

These devotions to the cross and other such religious exercises have lately fallen from favor. Excesses of sentimentality—to say nothing of maudlin art—are embarrassing to the contemporary mind. Still, we might grieve at the passing of such piety which at its best was a devotion to the cross of Christ and an inspiration to imitation of his life. These practices tended to offer the image of the cross as the essence of Christ. While it is true that one image is not the total entity, we are bereft if we deprive ourselves completely of such images. Recent emphasis on the communal nature of Christian worship has further demoted devotional practices which tend to be highly individualistic. Nonetheless, these devotions were one way that Francis' vision of the cross was kept alive among us. Francis was overwhelmed by the cross, his life altered by a crucifix, his body wounded by its nails. Such intense Christian experience should find ways to be sustained among us as well.

Since the death of Francis, more than three hundred people are said to have had an experience of the stigmata. Some have had actual wounds like those of Francis. Others have experienced excruciating pains in palms, feet and side. In some cases the stigmata appear and disappear; in others the manifestation is constant. How do such wounds and pains come to be? Are they self-inflicted? Are they real physical lesions given miraculously by God? Are they always the result of an ecstatic vision? What is the connection between these visions, physical debility and emotional imbalance? Does it matter? What about evidence that the nails of a crucified victim were usually hammered through the wrist, not the palms? Our penchant for scientific explanations for every phenomenon is confronted by the testimony of many who saw such wounds on Francis, and who explained them as a precious gift from God, testifying that likeness to Christ is the goal of every baptized Christian.

Reaching consensus about the origin of such phenomena is not the point. Christianity and, indeed, all world religions try to interpret the events of the world, natural and otherwise, in the truth of God. Christians see events in the light of Christ. The point of Francis' stigmata and of other similar experiences is incorporation into Christ, imitation of Christ as religious devotion, likeness to Christ as the worship of God. We may or may not wish to experience such religious ecstasy, but we should stand respectfully before those who have. We also seek in some way to be graced with a vision of God.

THEOLOGY OF THE CROSS

Lutherans are as devoted to the cross in their own way as Francis was in his. The television preacher Robert Schuller recently told some Lutheran seminarians that they talk too much about the cross. Indeed, "the theology of the cross" is a shorthand expression often used to characterize Lutheran theology. Martin Luther's vision of God was expressed verbally, intellectually, while Francis' was expressed dramatically, emotionally. Luther was a university theologian, not an itinerant troubadour, but Luther's vision of God was, like that of Francis, a vision of the cross. Jurgen Moltmann, a contemporary theologian, speaks of the "crucified God," using the same radical language which we know in Luther. "Apart from this man there is no God," wrote Luther regarding the humanity of God in the Crucified One. The Lutheran gift is to see the paradoxes present in Christianity, the throne of God as the cross on Calvary, the divine splendor as the crown of thorns, the light of god as the darkness of Good Friday. Lutherans take all religious language—God, splendor, life, goodness, holiness—and subject it to the cross, to the Crucified One and his death. When Luther interpreted all Scriptures through Christ, he found not some glorified demigod but a crucified man enlivening the words of Old and New Testaments alike.

Faithful devotion to the cross of Christ and to its reality in human life hindered Luther from closer association with some of the other Protestant Reformers. In characteristically blunt tones, Luther one day shouted in exaggeration, "I'd rather drink blood with the Pope than wine with the Swiss!" He meant that the sign of the cross still was revered as alive and salutary among both Roman Catholics and Lutherans of the sixteenth century. Our mutual devotion to the cross, whether expressed dramatically and emotionally or intellectually and theologically, remains one of the great bonds between Lutherans and Roman Catholics.

Lutherans are not devoid of devotional piety either. It is common for Lutherans to hold Lenten services in which the sign of the cross is exalted in hymns about the passion and portrayed artistically. Homilies about the passion figure prominently, making Lent a kind of communal way of the cross. A not uncommon name for Lutheran parishes is "Holy Cross." It is a custom to begin the school year in Lutheran parochial schools with an observance of the feast of the Holy Cross and its lessons of paradox. In the Lutheran hymnal, the famous Christmas carol "What Child Is This?" retains the original juxtaposition of the manger with the line, "Nails, spear, shall pierce him through/ The cross be borne for me, for you." That's very Lutheran—to recall the crucifixion and death of Jesus on Christmas, the celebration of his birth.

THE RECONCILING CROSS

Contemporary Lutherans and Roman Catholics stand together under the cross, like John and Mary, one writing paradoxical theology, the other adoring the body of Christ. The joy is that we stand there together, John and Mary, at the cross, our joy coming from the cross, our perfect joy in that cross. We live at a time when, standing there together, we are beginning to recognize one another, to call one another by name, to reverence one another, to respect one another's gifts. As joy is in Christ, so is reconciliation, not in official dialogues or in living room conversations. As the cross of Christ is reconciliation of the world to God, so is the cross our reconciliation with one another. The inspiration of Francis, the intercession of Francis, our discussions about Francis—these will not effect our reconciliation. Rather, that cross which gave Francis his inexplicable wounds and his greatest joy will achieve it.

The cross is one and the same for us. The cross signed at our baptism is one cross for all Christians. The cross preached in our sermons, the cross with which we are blessed each week, the cross with which our foreheads are marked, the cross which finally stands over our casket—this is one and the same cross for all of us. In a world increasingly pagan, the cross is sheer nonsense. Read Friedrich Nietzsche at the close of the last century leading our age in ribald mockery of the God of the cross. The differences between us seem increasingly unimportant compared with the overwhelming vision we share, seen in different guises, described in different ways, lived through different pieties: the vision of the Crucified One.

Francis' vision of the crucified one speaking at St. Damian shaped his life into holiness. His stigmatization began two years of ever intensifying mystical ecstasy. He drew away more and more from the world, closer and closer to God. The Christian is convinced that the way to God, the only effective path to heaven, is through the cross. The cross is the very sign of God on earth. We say with the emperor Constantine, "In this sign we shall conquer." In the thirteenth century, Franciscans began painting depictions of the cross as a bountiful tree, the fruit on the branches the saintly virtues. The cross is also our sign of the tree of life. That archetypal religious symbol of the great world tree, we Christians have found to be living still on Calvary. Together with Francis, we say, "By your cross you have redeemed the world."

9

C and P

IN THE SEDER FOUR CUPS OF WINE ARE RAISED. THE FIRST ONE SANC-
tifies the feast; the second accompanies the telling of the tale—
its volume of wine lessened by ten drops, ten drops given up
in sorrow for the sufferings of the Egyptians. The third cup, "the
cup of blessing," praises God for the meal and for salvation; and
the last cup, to anticipate the end time, cries out, "Next year in
Jerusalem!" Historians of liturgy like to see a connection between
the Jewish cup of blessing and the Christian cup of eucharist,
for at table with the disciples Jesus raised the cup after dinner
to bless God for salvation.

But there is yet a fifth cup, the cup of Elijah. It stands filled with wine at a place set for that great harbinger of God, because maybe, just maybe, this year, this Passover, God will come here, to our dinner table, in the divine messenger Elijah. At one point during the Seder ritual the door of the house is opened and the outside steps searched: Was that sound we heard possibly Elijah's knock? No, I can't see Elijah there after all. And sometime during the evening, perhaps as the children are searching for the hidden matzo, the cup gets mysteriously drained, and the children return to table to wonder whether God did, after all, send Elijah that year.

There is a way that we can see Elijah's cup as the one we Christians drain at the eucharistic meal. We can imagine that this holy cup is the one waiting through the ages to delight God's messenger, the draught which heralds the new age. Each eucharist is a celebration of the resurrection, each resurrection a Passover. This cup is reserved for and finally drunk by the one sent by God. It is as if we were sharing a meal of hope, and we opened the door because we thought we heard a knock; or perhaps the doors were locked for fear, and suddenly God has sent One to be at table with us. By this new Elijah the meal is sanctified as never before. God is present, and the meal has been transformed into a time of wonder. We add our experiences to the tales of long ago, and we tell the stories again: God shared dinner with Abraham at Mamre; God ate and drank with Moses and the elders; we knew him at the breaking of bread; Elijah's cup is drained, at this meal, by God.

"Are you able to drink the cup that I drink?" asks Jesus of his faithful ones. For there is also the cup of wrath:

> For in the Lord's hand there is a cup,
> full of spiced and foaming wine—the Lord pours it out—
> and all the wicked of the earth shall drink and drain the dregs.
> (Psalm 75)

Enraged Jeremiah demands that the world's evil ones be given the poisonous cup. Yet a stained-glass window in a Paris church depicts the winepress of God; intended to squeeze out the wine from the earth's sour grapes, it is instead pressing down on Christ, and his blood seeps out from his veins into the waiting chalices. And in the waiting room of an oncology surgeon in St. Paul, Minnesota, is a depiction of the Last Supper, the cup being filled with the tears of God and the bloody sweat of Jesus. For the drink poured for Jesus is not only the goblet of Elijah but also the vinegar of God's wrath and sorrow. "Abba, remove this cup from me," he begged.

Among the most revered of Christian artifacts have been the chalices, those great jeweled golden goblets, the ornate designs and engraved scenes fervently trying to make the outside of the cup worthy of its contents. But the wonder is not the spun silver depiction of Caleb and Joshua lugging back to camp a mammoth bunch of grapes, nor the gems which rivaled the sovereign's crown. The wonder is the wine of drinking the new covenant with God, the holy grail of the life of the one who drained the dregs of suffering. "Drink me," the bottle said to Alice: and so we do and, with Alice, are transformed. How impoverished they are who replace such a cup with glass jiggers, as if God were a sip, bottoms-up, a quarter-teaspoon measured out in the prescription of healing me! The four-year-old said, "It's funny: We drink God in the wine." Indeed, the finest, most precious article of our worship ought to be the cup, this container of God, which in pouring Christ into us all pours us into one another and so into God.

O Lord, you are my portion and my cup;
   in your presence there is fullness of joy,
   and in your right hand are pleasures for evermore.
                                                        (Psalm 16)

"The pinions of God will protect you."

P is for peacock, the paradise bird of stunning beauty, whose tail has a hundred eyes and whose flesh, it is said, does not decay. And so God is a peacock, immortality and glory and iridescent dress.

P is for pelican. The story says that in rage the father pelican murdered his young and that the mother pelican revived her children by sprinkling on them the blood she let from her own breast. In his hymn "Adoro Te," Thomas Aquinas recalls the myth by calling Jesus *pie pellicane.* (But Cardinal Newman edited that out, leaving Jesus only as the pure font.) And so God is a pelican, feeding her children with her own blood.

P is for phoenix. After living five hundred years on the tears of incense, the phoenix builds a death nest and sets itself on fire, from the ashes of which, three days later, emerges the new young phoenix; for there is only one phoenix alive at any one time. Its plumage is brilliant scarlet and gold. And so God is a phoenix, the only one, which offers itself for self-immolation and three days later is revived for life.

God's pinions: a nimbus shimmering blue-green; a bloody white breast; scarlet, then ash, then gold. A God with feathers? Divine plumes? Yet we sing, "Lord Jesus, since you love me, now spread your wings above me," and God describes the escape from Egypt as a flight on eagle's wings. That eagle flies through the psalms, the mother eagle pushing her young out of the nest to teach them to fly, but swooping down underneath to catch them with her wings in case they fall. Perhaps in the end-time authors and poets, still compulsively writing about the divine names, will be graced with a quill pen plucked from the plumage of God.

> Be merciful to me, O God, be merciful,
> for I have taken refuge in you;
>> in the shadow of your wings will I take refuge
>> until this time of trouble has gone by.[1]

(Psalm 57)

---

1. Quotations from the Psalms are drawn from the *Book of Common Prayer.* Used with permission.

10

Dancing around the Burning Bush

Words Dancing around the Fire

HOW DO WE TELL THE STORY OF MERCY TO ONE ANOTHER? PERHAPS there was first the isolated vision to the forebear. But even the solitary mystic, the crazed visionary, the lonely nomad, in seeing a vision of God, requires some set of human words to convey that vision to others. The prophets' ecstasy is tamed into coherent sentences, accessible even to the secular cynic. The otherworldly sighting of the divine selects simple words, stoops to a dictionary and a thesaurus, so that cradled in the right words the power of the extraordinary can be released to live anew. Exodus 3 is one such tale, ecstasy harnessed by grammar, the dream recorded, the vision ordered into narrative. For without such words the dream is only madness, the screams of the sibyl. Words shape the dynamism into a cup from which the whole community can drink divine life.

To speak of the divine encounter the sacred text uses the words and categories of the culture. God, goddess, Elohim: we begin where the language allows us a common noun. Exodus 3 relies on several such cultural categories of divine encounter. The estranged and tortured man receives a call; God is a tribal deity; God comes in a vision of fire; God is encountered on the mountain; God's name is revealed; the prophet is barefoot in humility; God's presence is marked by holiness; God promises blessings for the chosen people but punishment for the enemies of the people. This is all stereotypical religious stuff, the linguistic material for countless religious visions the world over. For even a unique vision, the words of description are borrowed from the holy words in the contemporary vocabulary.

Yet for this God, the God of Moses and of Jesus, these words do not set well. The sentences fail to tell the whole truth. The words can only dance around the fire. For example, the mountain is no stereotypical Mount Olympus, a mountain of God's abode where the pantheon chat and feast and deceive. Nor is this mountain even Mount Sinai, that high place of the Lawgiver breathing fire and smoke and commanding human responsibility. In Exodus 3 the mountain is Horeb: the bush is not consumed, and God promises to free the chosen people. Again in Exodus 17 the mountain of God is called Horeb, on which mountain God gives the people water from the rock to quench their thirst and to enliven their faith. Yet again in 1 Kings 19 the mountain of God, Horeb again, is the place to which Elijah flees from Jezebel and upon which he hears the divine voice in the stillness of a silent voice. Scholars say that Horeb is Sinai: yet interestingly the Horeb stories are narratives of grace, an unburning fire, flowing water, speaking silence. Exodus 3 relies on the age-old religious language of "the mountain of God" but bends it with mercy. The words dance around the old mountain talk to say new things of a new encounter with God.

The sentence describing the divine fire also strains the dictionary definition of the words. If it is a fire, why does it not burn? Is it a fire, or not? Instead of a monstrous conflagration, brimstone destroying Sodom, lightning obliterating Elijah's bull and altar, fire blazing away on Mount Sinai, we have instead a little bush, on fire yet not consumed. Our words try to speak of meeting God, but can only dance around some distance from the fire. So we meet a gracious God, who knows how dry and brittle we are, and so holds the divine majesty simmering gently in a bush so that we safely may gaze and wonder.

That our words cannot locate the divine center but can only dance around the fire is seen best in the giving of God's name. Volumes have been written on the possible meanings of these nouns and verbs: what is this name of God? We cannot get a firm grip upon it. Like fire it dances around in strange verb forms. Like the center of a flame, the vowel is missing. No matter how we set the vision into words, it sits wrong, or not quite right, like an appliqué of fabric flames sewn on a vestment and looking downright silly in its paltry depiction of flickering black and gold and red fire with flat orange felt. The name of God escapes our words.

Yet ours is not a religion for lonely visionaries and crazed hermits. The God of Jews and Christians is one of community. Thus the theophany must be told in words, some language chosen to attempt to pin down the flame. We gather around the words as around a campfire to know ourselves one in our common search for light and heat and to see ourselves united by the gift of divine light. That the narrative exists at all attests to our need for liturgy, the people's weekly assembly around word and sign as a way together to dance around the fire. The word in the flame unites Moses to his people, and in the telling of the words we are united to Moses and to all suffering people. The contemporary exegetes hear the fire calling their own given name and receive the call to become newly again members of a larger human community.

God Dancing in the Fire
We gather round the fire, for God is dancing in it. God is not only bellowing away in some volcanic explosion, belching out flames to consume the wicked. Here on Horeb God burns gently in the bush of the world, not to destroy it, but to call us by name and set us in community. Such naming gives us our identity, introduces us petulant hermits to our family, lays out our destiny of service, offers us mercy and assistance. Once the tree of life was guarded by the cherubim's flaming sword, fire keeping us from life. Yet here the image is reversed. The fire calls us to life, the flickering bush a strange tree of life centering our life in community in a gracious vision of God.

Yet in every age history attests that it is humankind who is in the fire. Cities—Troy, Jericho, Jerusalem, Hiroshima—continue to burn in memory, and their flames are rekindled daily. We burn away with one agony or another. Yet when the three faithful ones are thrown into Nebuchadnezzar's burning fiery furnace, God is in the furnace with them. This is our hope: God in the fire. Christians say it by proclaiming God on the cross, and by imaging Christ as the phoenix. Exodus 3 calls us to hope that even in Auschwitz God was with the chosen people in their suffering and that God wills for us all to be kept safe from such fires as will come. It is odd that in spite of the history of human terror we make comic stories of fires blazing away. Legend has it that when Lawrence the Deacon was martyred by being roasted on a grid, his last words were, "Turn me over, I'm done on that side." God must be seared on all sides, as are we all, for the flames rage unending through history. Yet we say God was in the flames first and remains therein with us.

The Dance

Joining hands around the fire we become the dance. No longer a refugee, a fugitive, a lonely man with a staff and some sheep: we become like the words themselves transfigured beings, awe-struck by God's power, united with those in the circle, called to make the circle wider. The lonely herdsman joins the dancing party. Jesus the shepherd becomes the lamb surrounded by the twelve gates and the 144,000 white-robed singers, the circles upon circles of those who take on their own light by reflecting divine light. No longer a pregnant teenager, estranged from her loved ones and afraid of the future: we become Mary's womb, nurturing the Christ child. We circle around God. Not even in the end-time do we become the divine Fire. We remain the dance around it, the townspeople gathering around the well, the five thousand eating remarkable bread on the hillside, the crowds dancing with the Torah down the street. We circle around the mystery of grace, sometimes cheering a man on a donkey, sometimes in silence attending a dying criminal, grateful for such meager words as have come down to us concerning the mercy of God.

ANALYZING
LITURGICAL LANGUAGE

11

Choosing the Words for the Church

WHICH WORDS SHOULD WE USE TO SPEAK TO AND OF GOD? DURING the last several decades Christians have asked this question repeatedly. The proliferation of biblical translations—a logical consequence of a century of historical critical studies—awakened us all to the intricacies of rendering ancient tongues in the vernacular. The revision of liturgical orders aroused the entire church catholic to the issues concerning appropriate prayer language. Academic studies of language and metaphor have taught liturgists new analytical skills. Christian feminists challenge our most comfortable formulas. From every room of the church we hear the question: which are the right words? What are the criteria for choosing the church's language? So far we have discovered only this: that far from reaching agreement with the committee across the hall, we cannot find consensus even among our own friends and colleagues, with whom with a shared zeal and for the common cause we discuss a single controverted phrase. We Pentecost people are in Babel-land.

We know that the church's language must continually change, because vernacular speech continuously changes. It is only rarely now that one comes across uninterrupted Latin or convincing Jacobean English. Yet we also know that our faith cannot willy-nilly discard its old vesture for brand new garb. Christianity is, among other things, a tradition of words, having a revealed name for God, a set of labels for holy things, certain categories for the self, and a vocabulary for the world. To pray in Christ is to use a certain set of words, and passing on the faith is to a great degree instruction in vocabulary: these are the words with which we pray, this is the song with which we praise, these sentences articulate what we profess. Thus changing the words of our prayer and praise is a momentous event, and it both signals and produces a revolution in the religious mind set. Yet words change out from under us, and we must keep on translating. In some cases the changes of the last decades were a move back out from the narrowness of a single tradition into the wider river of our origins. In other cases the changes prodded the church forward, urging us to reconcile our outmoded phrases with our contemporary sensibility. But since faithfulness to the tradition of holy words is an essential aspect of religion, we cannot so alter the vocabulary of the faith as to render it a new religion. For it was as primitive believers altered the Jewish vocabulary in essential ways, redefining words like Messiah, that Christianity was born. Rather, contemporary Christians whose task it is to choose the church's words seek to be faithful to the tradition of the cross and resurrection in the ever-changing words of their culture.

For we religious folk do hanker after the right words. What is your name, Moses asks God. Teach us to pray, plead the disciples. We laugh at the long footnote in Garrison Keillor's *Lake Wobegon Days* (New York: Viking, 1985; p. 107) which elucidates the splinter groups of his already miniscule religious tradition. Yet we devout students of Christian vocabulary are thereby smiling at ourselves. For we too care passionately about the meaning of the Scriptures; we too preserve zealously the spirit of our tradition; we too are apt to be most impatient with believers whose opinions are closest to our own. Most believers want to share their linguistic tradition with others, and even religious innovators who enjoy a private revelation from the divine quickly gather to themselves others who repeat the new holy words. For in the utter loneliness of the human self, religion's words give coherence to the world, meaning to chaos and death, answers to ultimate questions, indeed, the very questions worth asking. Religion bonds us to others, and for such united communion we humans require a shared vocabulary. Religion bonds us across time with the past and the future, and for such transtemporal experience the church seeks a constant vocabulary. Yet Christianity particularly is constantly in search of contemporary words, for we are a people of translation, Hebrew to Aramaic to Greek to Latin, and on and on, each language essential for the gospel for its time and place, yet yielding to translation to be faithful in another time and place. We who search for such a vocabulary are particularly harried these days, for our choices are many, the options myriad, the criteria unclear.

Throughout the church we can spot attempts to achieve linguistic certainty. The Roman Catholic Church has hoped to vest the magisterium with such authority. Thus Raymond E. Brown can delineate every possible interpretation of a biblical text and can then comment in a footnote that he believes that the meaning of a biblical phrase is what the Roman Church declared it to be. On the other hand, Protestantism has tried the opposite method: the individual Christian meditating on a select biblical translation can appropriate the language of faith. The last century has witnessed a fervor for fundamentalism unknown before in the history of the church, as lay Christians yearn for God's right words. The biblical scholar Martin Luther would be amazed and embarrassed at the biblical literalism that he could find in contemporary Lutheranism. But these familiar answers—the church knows the right words, the believer knows the right words, perhaps even the seminary knows the right words—are too simple: we are both "the church" and those Bible-reading believers, and we meet to admit that we do not know the words with which to pray. In our meeting we share our sorrow over those who, believing too precisely in a certain verbal formulation which has now been discarded, have given up—confused by the options, betrayed by the changes, bereft of any god bigger than the words they had been taught.

Our search for words that bear and reach God, that convey our ecstasy, that contain our longings, is for us an active endeavor. We are those who write the intercessory prayers, select the hymns, preach the sermons, instruct the children, lead the adult forums, and choose among Bible translations. Some of us are those who publish the church's prayers, who sit on translation committees, who argue for lectionary revision. It was folk like us who decided that "Sabaoth" was no longer the best word: not only did the vast number of faithful confuse it with Sabbath, but even Hebrew scholars thought that translating the image of God at the head of a host of heavenly armies failed in the contemporary world to be a metaphor for God's strength. It is as if we are curators of ecclesiastical museums and must once a decade encase behind glass a metaphor that no longer lives, words that can no longer speak truly of Christ in the assembly. That chalice is quaint, but it leaks, we say, and we retire from our use a certain container of holiness. Yet we are also archeologists, finding glorious vibrancy buried alive in long-abandoned texts and images. Ah, but how to choose? How to agree on the choices? The confession of sin prior to the eucharist provides us with one such example of a traditional metaphor which needs careful contemporary analysis. Let us consider for a moment what we mean by the confession of sin.

Religion suggests that God offers humankind the solution to its dilemma, and in the church's version of this religious expectation there have been at least three different ways to talk about the human dilemma. All three are justifiable expositions of biblical themes. There is, first, death. Adam and Eve are deprived of the fruits of the tree of life; humankind is not to live forever. Here is the primitive, rudimentary terror in the face of death. We will die, and we are afraid of death. Mortality before divinity implies death, and the Hebrews were sure that looking upon God brought on death. How can we live in spite of death? How can we live on after death? The hope for an heir and the promise of the land are Old Testament metaphors answering this fear of death. In the resurrection of Christ we see the Christian answer to this human dilemma; we will live again, as Christ did, after death. The eastern church has developed this set of words in its stress on divinization. We shall become divine, unconquered by death.

But the western church has spoken much less of divinization than of justification. For the story of the human fall has also been explicated to mean that the fundamental human dilemma is sin. We are cursed for preferring ourselves to God and our ways to God's ways, but God promises salvation. God will justify us and reconcile us back to grace. The death of Christ as atonement for sin provides the answer to the human dilemma when it is seen as sin. Paul's and Augustine's explorations in the guilty self-reflective consciousness set the west down this path, and the western medieval church trod these words—sin, justification, penance, repentance—nearly to extinction. Luther as a medieval Christian focused especially on this metaphor for the Christian faith, and the Reformation churches inherited his interest in sin as the primary human problem.

There is yet a third set of words articulating human ill, common in primitive Christianity, and it springs from messianic expectations and echoes the language of apocalypticism. According to this set of words, our worst problem is evil: oppression, injustice, systemic social ill. The longing for a messiah to establish a new order and our hope for heaven, a perfected existence, express the faith that with God's help evil can be vanquished and love can abound. Contemporary liberation theologies—black, Marxist, feminist—develop this set of words, seeing in Christ the way to a new world. Here it is not so much that I fear my death or that I anguish under a guilty conscience, but that daily we live nearly overwhelmed by evil. We take into ourselves the victims of the Holocaust. We search the past and future for vindication from God greater than the horrendous evil we humans can produce, and we unite in our baptism, standing alive with God's grace, to bring on the dominion which God has promised.

Against this background, let us consider the confession of sin. Our present attachment to this ritual involves a choice for a certain set of words. When we schedule the confession, we choose to continue among us preference for sin-and-forgiveness language. In doing so we must however continue the critical task: is this language the best—for surely it is not the only—to articulate the human problem and God's solution? Could it be that we take comfortable refuge in our guilty consciences and thus avoid greater problems of evil? How can the other categories of death and evil find expression in our liturgies? Yet as we in the west continue to regard justification as a primary category, we are required to continue analyzing its inherent ideas, for there is no consensus in the church today about what all human sin is. What gives one Christian an anguished conscience strikes another Christian as a gift of God's grace; and it is not clear whether the one burdened or the one free is more ethically Christian. It is hoped that the ecumenical liturgical consensus can teach us all a balance of words, so that while it would be irresponsibly self-congratulatory to dismiss sin as a western category, a focus on our puny sin does not so monopolize Christianity as to leave no energy for the questions of death and the reality of sin. An example of this balance can be seen in the current attempt to broaden the focus of Lent from a narrow obsession with guilt to a wider investigation of the baptized life in the face of death, sin, and evil.

The word *king* provides us with a second example of the word choices before us. Here the issue is not of choices among different metaphors, but of the translation of a key biblical metaphor into contemporary American English. When the nomadic tribes settled in Canaan and observed their neighboring urban cultures, the Hebrew people began to call out for a king. The patriarchal tribal system developed into a culture of the unified people under the single patriarch, the king. In this process the people's religious language began to call God king also, thus to affirm that the nation's king was a descendant of the king of the universe. The Jews continued to look for God's anointed one, the king. Sometimes the metaphor of God as king or the anointed one as king was explicated literally, as if the people of God would one day constitute a free state. Other interpretations suggest that the anointed king would establish a spiritual dominion. Christians have continued the ancient religious tradition of calling God king and as well have named the crucified one Christ, their anointed king. Christians perpetuate both the spiritualizing interpretation—the king not of this world—and the literal hope that an eschatological reign of God will renew the earth.

In the third line of the *Gloria in excelsis* we Christians call God king. The contemporary question is: Is this the best word to convey this complex history of metaphor? Of course, as in all metaphor, God was not ever really a king; the word was always a strange incongruous image. But especially in a democracy in which the images of the king and the queen are either charming nostalgia trips, glimpsed alongside the Tower of London, or signs of an antiquated political system, we must inquire whether our word king is big enough. Translating *melek* and *basileus* "Sovereign" at least eliminates the masculine limitation and perhaps will discourage petty artists from belittling our churches with inconsequential pictures of an old bearded crowned head. Yet should we choose to retain the masculine word for Jesus—"This is the king of the Jews"—we have lessened the Christological shock of applying all the titles of God to the man Jesus. The bitter truth is that in choosing religious language one feels like the city council deciding on curbs: replacing the curb with a ramp helps those in wheelchairs, but blind people walk out into the traffic. How can we declare that Jesus is God without implying that God is masculine? How can we laud Christ as king on Calvary without limiting God by an archaic metaphor? Which concern should we serve when?

The question of "king" illustrates the two tasks before us. First there is the decision of whether the biblical or traditional translation is still a living metaphor. That is, many common words are in fact dead metaphor. We are no longer surprised that a chair has a leg. The recent decision to drop "Sabaoth" from the *Sanctus* was based on a judgment that Sabaoth contained a dead metaphor that did not merit resuscitation. Many contemporary biblical translations abandon the Hebrew metaphor "to know" as a circumlocution for sexual intercourse, judging it (unfortunately?) a dead metaphor. Our religion must be filled with living metaphors. The metaphor of shepherd: is it still viable, capable of conveying the kerygma? The image of "Son of man" is an example of a metaphor not so much dead as gravely ill; repeatedly one hears the term explicated incorrectly. For Paul the Torah was no longer able to express God's grace; it was no longer a living metaphor for salvation. But for contemporary devout Jews, the law is God's greatest gift to humankind; see for example *Holy Days* (New York: Summit, 1985), the recent study of Hasidic Judaism by Lis Harris. For these believers the Torah is still a living metaphor of divine life. With whom lies the responsibility of choosing which are the living metaphors?

One such example of the question of living metaphor is the New Testament word *adelphoi* ("brothers" or "brethren" in RSV). In different contexts and as used by different New Testament writers, this word can mean the disciples, the hearers of a speech, the members of a male group, the adult members of a specific Christian assembly, the Christian community as a whole, those sharing a specific fate. Should current translations render all these groups with the same word? Which overtones of the word *adelphoi* should we retain—the masculine, the familial, the communal? Do we translate the word differently in different contexts? When is merely adding "and sisters" the best solution, and when is that inaccurate and irresponsible translation? Is there a better word altogether? Here is the question: What is the living metaphor essential to our faith in the New Testament metaphor "brothers"?

Once we decide which are the living metaphors, our second task, a mammoth one, is laid before us. We must instruct the faithful in the meaning of the words. We must teach the children who David was so that the term Christ can have some meaning. We must connect for them Samuel's anointing of David, the meaning of "the Messiah," and their own baptismal anointing. We must tell the stories of washing and eating so that our sacramental practice will have the imaginative foundation for which it begs. The renewed popularity of Jesse trees in Advent and Christmas, over against the trees of apples-and-bows of my childhood, shows a return to the images of the tradition, to all the sacred stories, so that our celebration of the incarnation can be filled with yet deeper meaning. Again we are reading the mystagogical catechesis of the early centuries of the church and are trying a contemporary hand at the skill: how can the baptized grow deeper into the meaning of the words of their faith? The metaphors which are worth keeping alive become the focus of our catechesis and the vehicle for our preaching.

Yet this is not all. There is also, first and last, the fundamental concern for the artistry of our language. It is simplistic to claim that in the olden days the church employed language of beauty and that in recent decades this requirement has been abandoned. Rather, Latin and Jacobean English, languages which were too smoothly cadenced to contain contemporary reality, have been laid aside. Admittedly the committee prose of typical recent liturgical revision has seldom given us the power of ecstatic speech, the vibrance of great poetry, the oxymorons of a sensibility that has confronted God. The prayers of our recent service orders have not been great enough. But even though they are too sparse and brittle, we have many occasions in any particular liturgy to incorporate impassioned language, words stunned by the vision of God. Weekly there is the selecting of hymns, the training of lectors, the crafting of sermons, the shaping of prayers. We can clean up our bulletin of ugly language: "Pairs and Spares will meet Thursday nite," for instance. We must consider the damage done by representing in the bulletin the worship of God's people as if it were a book's Table of Contents correctly paginated. Perhaps the next few decades will afford to the ecumenical liturgical consensus many occasions in which to improve on the artistry of our speech toward God and one another.

Choosing our words is no different from renovating our churches. Some of the artifacts have long since lost any religious power they ever had—although one wonders what all those ascending feet of Christ on all those altar paintings ever said about the vital presence of a living Christ in the church. Out they go. Other of the artifacts need cleaning or repair: after a decade of burlap with elementary school felt glue-ons, perhaps we are glad we saved the simple brocade frontal. (Ah, but if it only didn't have "Holy Holy Holy" written on it in obsolete lettering, as if holiness could be spelled, and required an old-fashioned pen.) Other artifacts—the word Hosanna, or a return to historic vestments—need catechesis, that we can experience their meaning anew. Some new things will enter the liturgy, choices now for now; who knows how long they will remain? The canons and chants of the Taizé community may be with us one generation or for the rest of the church's life, for the choices in the liturgy will go on.

It would be heartening if we could process down the mountain with all the right words emblazoned into tablets of stone. But even Moses had to go back a second time. And when we have the words—Jesus reading from Isaiah in the synagogue—we are given a strange meaning for the words, a Jewish itinerant preacher proclaiming that there in Nazareth is alive and thriving the very dominion of God. What did the writer of Isaiah mean by those words? What did Jesus mean? What did Luke mean? How do we cast it in contemporary American English? How do we preach it as God's good news for me and for the world? What has it to do with death, with sin, and with evil?

If you get any of these answers, be sure to let me know.

12

Blessing God with Bread and Wine

EVEN AS PROTESTANTS ARE REINTRODUCING THE EUCHARISTIC PRAYER into the liturgy, there still remains some hesitancy born of the Reformation rejection of the prayer and its action. We recall that Martin Luther threw out the prayer, saying dreadful things about its medieval content. The Reformers saw in the prayer a sacrifice offered by the priest: and both the idea of the eucharist as sacrifice and the power of the medieval priest were objects of Protestant criticism. Indeed, the fact that our word "hocus-pocus" evolved from the parishioners' garbled version of *Hoc est corpus meum* ("This is my body") indicates that whatever was going on during the prayer was misunderstood by many Christians for several centuries. Yet the eucharistic prayer, its content and its action, is simple praise of God. The assembly praises God—blesses God, we say—uniquely in the eucharistic liturgy and especially in that great thanksgiving prayer. But the prayer blesses God with bread and wine, and this is where the confusion arises. What does it mean to bless God with bread and wine?

Let us begin by examining the fundamental word "bless." In the first place, blessing is a divine action. It is done by God to the chosen. The salvation history of Israel is a tradition of whom God blessed, and of how God gives life, God saves the people, God blesses Abraham, Isaac, and Jacob. Secondly, we pray that God will bless others. May the LORD bless and keep you, the presider says in the Aaronic blessing (Numbers 6:24–26). Ritually important figures like priests and cultural authorities like patri-

97

archs had the right to convey that blessing of God on others. So
Isaac blesses Jacob. Because of their position, their plea for God's
blessing had effective power.

But in Deuteronomy 8:10, and constantly in the psalms we
bless God. That is, we acclaim the life of God. We call out to
earth and heaven that our God is the one who is life and who
gives life. Our praise of God, our blessing God, is our affirmation
that God is the one who has the power of life; God is the one
who owns the right of blessing. "The LORD will bless us. . . .
May you be blessed by the LORD. . . . But we will bless the
LORD from this time forth and for evermore," sings Psalm 115,
verses 12, 15, and 18 using the word bless in its various forms.
The Hebrew word *berak* describes the reciprocal relationship of
the covenant: God gives us life, and we give God praise; God
blesses us, and we bless God.

Now in religious ritual we bless God not only with our voices
and our songs. We use natural and crafted objects in our blessing
of God. For example, we bless God with the organ. That is, the
organ joins us in praise; it assists our praise; it objectifies our
praise; it symbolizes our praise. In Psalm 103 and in St. Francis'
famous Canticle of Brother Sun the whole created order praises
God; and with the holy universe, the universe made whole in
God, we join in blessing.

Taking a cue from 1 Chronicles 17:27, "What you, O LORD,
have blessed is blessed for ever," we say of these objects with
which we have blessed God that they themselves are blessed.
By this we do not mean that objects have a magical power in
themselves. We mean instead that these objects join us in praising God. Already in the second century Hippolytus' church order
indicates blessing formulas not only for bread and wine, but also
for oil, cheese, olives, milk with honey, and water for drinking.
But Hippolytus wrote in his list of blessings, "But in every blessing shall be said, 'To you be glory, to the Father and to the Son
with the Holy Spirit in the holy church, now and forever, world
without end.'" To bless bread and wine, oil and cheese means
to use these objects to bless God in the church.

Melchizedek gives us an image with which to apply the word
bless. In Genesis 14:18–20 Melchizedek, the king of Salem and
priest of God Most High (interesting: not God YHWH), blesses
God for salvation, acclaims that Abram has been blessed by God,

and ritually offers bread and wine. The writer of the Hebrews (ch. 7) uses Melchizedek as a metaphor for Christ: Christ comes as priest and king, blessing God, blessing us by God, and offering bread and wine. The blessing from God comes to us through the mediation of the one king and priest Christ. Christ bears the blessing of God, and so we are blessed, as we join with Christ to bless God, offering bread and wine. In the mosaics in Ravenna and throughout Christian iconography Melchizedek is not only a metaphor for Christ but also for the presider at the eucharist who in offering to Abram and to us bread and wine seals the covenant of blessing with God. The bread and wine sign for us wholeness with God, God's blessing of us and our blessing of God.

In the eucharistic prayer we bless God with bread and wine. This great thanksgiving prayer is most likely derived from the *Birkat-ha-Mazon*, the Jewish meal prayer. Christians praise God especially for the person of Christ, crucified and alive again and present uniquely in this very meal. Remembering the salvation given us in Christ, we offer the bread and cup with our praise. In remembrance of Christ we praise God, we pray this prayer, we offer ourselves, and we offer bread and wine with our praise. As the Common Eucharistic Prayer has it, "We now celebrate this memorial . . . Recalling Christ's death . . . and offering to you this bread and this cup, we praise you and we bless you."

Clearly, the old designation of this prayer as the consecration prayer suggested that the words of the prayer effected the consecration of the elements. Thus arose interminable arguments about a moment of consecration, in which some specific words spoken by the presider functioning quite like magic changed bread into body, or added the body to the bread, or made the symbolism effective. The move to suppress the name "consecratory prayer" indicates contemporary thought that such notions misinterpret the eucharistic prayer and misunderstand Christian praise. The prayer is far from magical formula: the prayer is praise of God for the person of Christ, and like Melchizedek of old and the host at Jewish meals, Christians offer their praise with bread and wine. The bread and wine—symbols of God's creation, human industry, our sustenance and our joy— join us in our praise. We say they too are blessed, made holy by providing for our liturgy the mode for the presence of Christ among us.

But we are Christians, and our pattern of praise, learned from the Jews, bends in a new way around the cross. As we receive the bread and the cup, words are spoken to seal our faith that in our praise of God, Christ has been made known. "The body of Christ, the blood of Christ": and we say Amen. Here we have not even full sentences, no verbs, only the language of faith, language used strangely. The bread does not look like body, the wine does not taste of blood. This is not the language of labels but the language of metaphor: not metaphor as image contrary-to-fact, but metaphor as religious reality, the world seen anew by the power of the resurrection. The bread is not changed to body, nor does the bread represent the body: both verbs, change and represent, are too weak to articulate our faith that in this act, in our praise of God with our offering of bread, the body of Christ is manifest among us. Jews praise God, and we join them in praise; but our baptism teaches us to say that Christ is made known in that breaking of bread.

The church is always trying to explain what happens to the bread and wine during or because of this prayer. Much of church history is the continuous argument over which contemporaneous terms best say our faith in the real presence of Christ in the eucharist. Ecumenical reconciliation is perhaps best achieved not by continuing to martyr one another over old designations but by searching together in contemporary philosophy for language to articulate the mystery of our sacred bread. Edward Schillebeeckx is leading the way in his use of contemporary phenomenology.[1] He proposes that we think of personal encounter as constitutive of our perception of reality. We do not think of things really out there which perhaps we observe well or ill, as did medieval philosophy. Instead we think of human perception—thus also interpersonal encounter—as constituting the only reality of which we can speak. Christ is really present in the eucharist: that is, in these created forms God gives us the person of Christ, and our communal reception of Christ among us constitutes the eucharist. The bread and wine are signs of the

1. Edward Schillebeeckx, *The Eucharist*, trans. N.D. Smith (NY: Sheed and Ward, 1968).

parousia already, a beginning here and now of life transfigured by the resurrection. Perhaps ecumenical conversation over these proposals can hasten consensus among us.

Not only our words but even our gestures indicate our faith in the presence of Christ in the meal. The presider stands in the ancient Hebrew posture of praise, arms extended toward the skies, as if the arms could project the praise through human failure up to God's throne. Yet the fathers said that the arms should be somewhat lower, not as if reaching the clouds but as if pinned to a cross. Again the Jewish pattern of prayer is altered by the crucifixion. The very *orans* position is a metaphor for our faith that in our praise of God Christ is revealed.

The assembly stands during this Great Thanksgiving. Medieval practice urged that the faithful kneel in their reverence at the sudden appearance of the Monarch of Heaven and Earth in the room. But contemporary Christians have returned to ancient practice that the baptized assembly stands boldly before God, upright after the descent into the font, Ezekiel's resurrected bones now a standing army before the LORD. We stand, not before a great throne, not before a sacred shrine, but around a table. For Christians, the praise of God begins and ends at a table. The disciples of Emmaus recognized the resurrected Lord in the breaking of bread, and in the Apocalypse's vision of the court of God, a lamb hosts a great victory feast. We stand around the bread and wine to praise God, and with us stand the angels and the saints of old who join in our song of praise.

But although we stand around a table, we reverence bread and wine as we reverence the LORD in our midst. Mark 5 contains the long narrative of the hemorrhaging woman who is healed by touching the hem of Jesus' garment. Jesus perceives "that power had gone forth from him," and he searches for the one who touched him. But Matthew gives this story a different treatment. He edits out all of Jesus' acknowledgement of the holiness of his garment. The woman tries to touch his hem, but Jesus intervenes and, commending her faith, heals her. Furthermore, Matthew places this pericope directly after Jesus' teaching (Mt 9:14–17) about the new garments. He warns that we are not to put new patches on old garments, but get ourselves new garments altogether, new wineskins. Perhaps Matthew on purpose juxtaposes these stories: Christ is a whole new garment we are to put on. It is not that Christ's garment is holy. His clothes do not grant healing: he does. So in the eucharist, the bread and wine are not some kind of relics, leftovers from the presence of God, something made holy and thus holy for our touch. The bread and wine are the presence of Christ for us, and, believing, we are made whole.

In the eucharistic prayer we bless God with the bread and wine. The eucharistic prayer is thus a metaphor for our whole baptized life in which we praise God with all that we have and make. We stand in the assembly, under that picture of old Melchizedek, and bless God for the person of Christ. In such worship we know the bread and ourselves to be the body of Christ, and we await the eschaton, when all the world will know it.

13

Teaching Children the Words of Faith

ECUMENICAL EXCITEMENT CONCERNING ADULT BAPTISM IS PRODUCING a good deal of literature on adult catechesis. Renewed models take into account that amendment of life as well as intellectual knowledge reflects baptismal grace, and that the pattern of the academic year is hardly the most appropriate structure for mystagogy. It is not surprising, however, to discover that sometimes material designed for adult catechesis can work against a healthy catechesis for children. The notion of the Christian as a literate, intelligent, responsible free agent can give a shape to Christian instruction that leaves little room for small children.

While *metanoia* is an appropriate primary metaphor for an ongoing conversion to the life of faith, it is not a particularly helpful one when we focus on the preschool or primary school child. Most likely this child has neither a demonic past to abandon nor a disciplined self-reflective consciousness with which to contemplate sin and grace. For the young child the experience must be of nurture and familial embrace; the appropriate image is not so much drinking from the thanksgiving cup as it is nursing on God's milk. Catechesis for the child parallels the biblical story of Jacob's ladder. Contrary to the presentation in the popular ballad, Jacob did not, as some free and forgiven adult, climb the ladder; rather, the angels of God descended the ladder to bless the sleeping and helpless son.

This essay takes for granted several premises, none of them universally accepted; there is space here only to state them

103

clearly. The first premise is that normally infants of believing parents ought to be baptized into the church. A second premise is that the interior life of even very small children is far more receptive and complex than many adults assume. A third is that faith is more than a conscious adult act; it is also an unconscious predisposition for life, an attitude of trust like that which Erik Erikson postulates as the normal acquisition of the first year of life. Even the smallest child, therefore, can genuinely share in the life of faith.

A fourth premise is that baptized children, whether infants, toddlers, preschoolers, or primary school children, belong weekly at the holy eucharist with their families. At times being in church will include—more or less for various children—being in the narthex, temporarily separated from the main body of the community while restlessness and tears are overcome. But the narthex is a place of waiting to get back into the church to focus again on God; thus it is wholly different from the nursery, a place of play and focus on the child. Attention to God is not a particularly easy skill to master at any age, but it is not defensible to suggest that such an attitude can be postponed until adulthood. *The Sacred Play of Children*, a collection of essays edited by Diane Apostolos-Cappadona (Seabury, 1983), offers much wisdom on this question of the place of children at the church's weekly liturgy.

This essay seeks to suggest some catechetical implications for the baptized and regularly worshiping child. The suggestions assume that the children normally experience their Christianity within the full community. Even in extraordinary circumstances like institutions and children's wards, it is advisable somehow to include adults in the primary religious experience of the children. If children are normally segregated in worship, they can only conclude that what they are experiencing is kids' stuff which mercifully they will outgrow.

Granting the weekly corporate experience, there are still many occasions when catechesis can be designed especially for a specific age group. Home devotional life, Sunday church school, and religious training in parochial schools are some examples. Our task is to discern the catechetical principles for this instruction that proceed logically and theologically from the child's baptism.

Praying and Praising

Catechesis is baptismal instruction. That is, it is instruction in the paschal life for the baptized or the about-to-be-baptized. The most essential component of catechesis is instruction in prayer and praise. We who are baptized are called to worship God, and every small event of prayer and praise can nurture our continuing growth in worship. Thus, we invite small children to new moments of prayer: we hold the infant's hands together and repeat "Abba, Amen"; we recite with the toddler a short poem to God, and exchange with the preschooler such classic Christian phrases as "This is the day the Lord has made" and "Lord, open my lips."

It is important that, even at a very young age, the child learns to view prayer as something greater than a list of personal requests and God-bless-mommys. One of the goals of catechesis is to widen and deepen the child's prayer concern. To pray for hungry children, for children without heat or fans, and for children in hospitals draws the child out of self-centered prayer and into the love for one another to which the church calls all its members.

Teaching children pieces of the church's historic liturgy (i.e., "Guide us waking, O Lord, and guard us sleeping . . .") also enriches their vocabulary and so, gradually, the theology of children's prayer. Experimenting with little used or innovative images for God gives their religious imagination an occasion to picture a greater God in newer ways.

It is also important not to forget praise. The bedtime or classroom litanies need not always be petitionary; we can vary them with acclamations of the form, "For _____, we praise you, O God!" Even the smallest children can learn some classic hymns of the Christian faith and thus expand their language of faith. Hand motions, which we can coordinate not only with "Gospel Light" but also with "Now thank we all our God" and other classics, enable youngsters to involve their whole bodies in the praise of God.

Never should moments of children's devotion be seen as replacements for the church's liturgy. Children's devotions are grounded in the language and experience of the wider church, and at their best they prepare the child to return to church next week. Above all, catechesis can in no way be conceived apart from prayer and praise. It is not that we need more and better children's homilies to teach children about faith. Rather, what we are always learning—preschooler and granddaddy mystic alike—is how to pray.

Learning the Story

Catechesis for the young child ought to consist mainly of the stories of the faith. The old-fashioned Sunday school leaflet had much going for it. A few publishing houses offer fine bible story collections with good illustrations for daily home reading. I recommend Paulist's *A Child's Bible* and the Taizé Bible.

I judge a fine bible story collection to be one in which the stories are told as biblically as possible with as many details as the child's age allows. Small children are not concerned with the actual location or date of events or even with the "meaning" of the story; but they are interested in exactly what Joseph's long-sleeved, many-colored coat was like. I judge a bible story collection in which Pharaoh is discussing his need for Hebrew slaves with his wife who is lying in bed with curlers in her hair to be worse than worthless.

Why the stress on bible stories? Quite simply, children love stories, and their early knowledge of first a few and then the many stories of faith will give them the best foundation possible for life in the church. Use these years to tell and retell the lives of the saints. Rather than lecture a high school student on the meaning of the title "messiah," read a small child the stories of the good and bad kings of Israel. Rather than laboriously teach a confirmation class about the anthropology of food, tell toddlers the stories of Abraham at Mamre and the two disciples (perhaps one was a woman) at Emmaus.

The ancient church called this method of biblical instruction typology. While it is essential that biblical scholars move beyond this and utilize the full range of historical and critical tools, typology still works well to incorporate the small child into the stories of faith.

Take, for example, the sensational Elijah stories, which children love. The youngest child can simply hear the wondrous story. But already the kindergartener can be drawn into the paschal meaning of the story. Elijah and the widow can be an image of the eucharist. The healing of the widow's son can be a picture of our baptism and our life in God. The contest with the prophets of Baal is rich with possibilities: the altar—we ourselves—doused with water three times and gifted by the fire of God's Spirit. The still small voice opens us to honesty about the life of faithful prayer in the face of fear—a powerful image for every young child who is afraid of the monsters of the night. Such a method of instruction focuses on the stories' wonderful details, rather than subsuming the details into a grand historical or theological scheme which cannot interest the small child.

Maturing in Morals

We worship God and stand with the forerunners of the faith, and so we live renewed lives. Already for small children, obedience to God is a component of faith. Of course, "being good" ought never be equated with the Christian life. Such an equation is patently untrue and can be extremely detrimental to children's religious growth. But as the child learns to pray, to praise, and to live in the light of the stories of faith, Christian catechesis can also point the way to appropriate behavior for the renewed life. Biblical narratives, however, should seldom, if ever, be used expressly as object lessons for behavior. Such a technique usually distorts the biblical story beyond recognition; even worse, it trains the children to think of biblical applications in a way that they will later see as inadequate or even erroneous.

The best way to help the child mature in Christian morals is to be attuned to the questions of right and wrong that are on the child's mind and to deal sensitively with those issues at the time. Abstract rules tend to help neither small children nor sophisticated adults. While it is important for older children to know the classic commandments, specific conversation about "What is a lie?" or "Whom can we hate?" assists the child who is wrestling with concrete instances of these moral dilemmas on the road to Christian maturity. My six-year-old, for example, was fascinated by the story of Rahab, who is praised and even saved for lying.

Christian ethicists struggle valiantly over moral issues, and even the small child can be shown some of the process involved in responsible Christian decision. Rather than deduce morals from bible stories, it is better to recall bible stories at the time the moral question is a live one for the child. Then the child concretely faces the fundamental questions: What does one's baptism mean for one's response to this situation? How does one who bears the name of Jesus act in such a moment?

Children are as different from one another as are adults. Some are overly afraid of doing wrong and need to be freed by their baptism to take risks. Others blithely sail through sin and need to be recalled by their baptism to obedience. That is why a detailed prescription for moral instruction is so difficult. Only a sensitive, attentive parent or teacher can discern and shape what is most helpful in each specific situation.

Recently, after a hiatus of many years, I met the pastor who baptized me as a six-week-old infant. A circle of people gathered around us and raised their glasses "to the baptism that really took." What the grace of that baptism began, years of catechesis nurtured. Into that water rained meal prayers and night prayers, daily bible reading, *Little Visits with God*, weekly church services, midweek Lenten services, Sunday school, Christian day school, vacation bible school, confirmation, and the model of devout parents. It was a veritable hailstorm of catechesis; and it is perhaps consoling to add that most of this catechesis occurred within parish contexts that were far from ideal. Fortunately the milk of God keeps flowing, ready to fill us and our children, beyond and outside even our highest expectations.

14

The Poetic Nature of Liturgical Language

UNTIL THE TWENTIETH CENTURY, IT WAS RELATIVELY EASY TO DISTIN-guish between English prose and English poetry. Prose and poetry were specific literary forms that were distinct from one another. A novel was a novel, a sonnet a sonnet. Words were arranged into a form, and if one knew the definitions of the forms, identification was self-evident. Even the bizarre *Tristram Shandy* is clearly a novel, blank pages, line drawings, nonsensical excurses, and aborted plot notwithstanding. If words were arranged in a poetic form but so poorly as to defame the word "poetry," we called that "verse"; but verse, as a subclass of poetry, was not confused with prose. Form was all.

The business of making distinctions is more difficult in this century. Much modern poetry creates its own form, one perhaps unrecognizable to the newcomer. Few poems adhere to classic forms. What makes poetry into poetry these days is not adherence to a form, but rather the degree to which words are used metaphorically rather than discursively. That is to say: although you arrange directions on how to assemble a bookshelf into blank verse, you do not have a poem. You have prose with studied line lengths. The intent of the language and the use of the words is narrative, discursive, logical. The words are used primarily—perhaps exclusively—to convey a single unambiguous meaning, with the hopes that even the dullest consumer will correctly assemble the bookshelf.

On the other hand, when words are used primarily meta-phorically, we have poetry, regardless of line lengths, rhymes, or beat patterns. Poetry is the tension produced by talking about two things at the same time. The metaphor of poetry implies ambiguity. A careful reader perceives that the assembly instructions are not at all about putting together a bookshelf: They are really about my failed love affair! Prose may employ metaphoric language, figures of speech, to enlighten the sentences, but poetry is in the first place an intense interplay of words which are metaphor for its own sake. Although Faulkner piles words upon words into page-length sentences of growing intensity, he is primarily narrating a plot. So we say that Faulkner writes prose. Compare with James Joyce's opening of *Finnegans Wake*:

> riverrun, past Eve and Adam's, from swerve
> of shore to bend of bay, brings us by a commodius
> vicus of recirculation back to Howth Castle and
> Environs.

This has more to do with poetry than with prose.

Theology is prose. It attempts to organize an array of thoughts about God into a coherent system. It presents logical—or at least consistent—definitions for obscure human and divine phenomena. Christian theology is also exposition of biblical texts, discursive discussion toward cogent understanding. Theological writings aim for lucidity, and while not all theology succeeds, the attempt is there, by definition.

I was raised in a tradition that has high regard for theology—at least its own theology. The Bible is revered and memorized especially as it authenticates a certain theological system. Such theological precision of course has enormous values.

However, in my tradition, the liturgy as well was solely a vehicle for theology. We memorized theological hymns of ten stanzas that explain meticulously the distinction between law and gospel. Rubrics too had solely theological purpose. Whether the presider faced the wall or the people was mandated by definitions of "prayer" and "proclamation," that is, action toward God or actions toward the people; and of course every part of the liturgy could be labeled exclusively one or the other. Within such concern for theological precision, the liturgy is seen as prose, a kind of (usually) spoken dialogical sermon in which pastor and people share in a weekly recitation of theological beliefs. Liturgy is creed. Subjectivism is anathema, since feelings tend to overflow their bounds. Poetry is feared, since blurred meanings confuse the authority of language.

Notwithstanding my rearing, I now reckon liturgy as poetry. The liturgy is not primarily a discursive dialogue that outlines coherent facts about faith. It is rather a sustained metaphor in which language, body, movement, music, architecture, and art simultaneously play on biblical, traditional, and contemporary images and themes in an effort—never totally successful, always flawed and partial—to receive God in the world. It is not surprising that the stories tell of people struck dumb or dead at the sight of God. Nor is it surprising that theology must continually write and rewrite its discursive logic in an attempt to articulate God. For it cannot be done, humans capturing the divine. For this reason Mary is such a wonder, for there is a way in which, uniquely among humans, she contained God. At best we have the liturgy, the attempt which must by metaphor stand at the base of Jacob's ladder as the angels descend to bless us.

What do I mean, liturgy is poetry? On the simplest level I mean what everybody knows, that there is much poetry used in the liturgy. The psalms are poetry, seen since the origin of the church as the essential resource for Christian worship. The psalms are poetry not primarily because they are Hebrew poems with patterns of parallel structure and recurring beats, but because they are, in Hebrew and in English, sustained religious metaphors. Patristic preaching knew this when it saw in all sorts of psalm metaphors an image of Christ. God is a rock, a refuge, a king, a shepherd, a tower, a song. We are so accustomed to some of these metaphors—God as king, for example—that we forget that they are just that, metaphors. Perhaps the psalms which describe human pain as our being attacked by wild dogs or being surrounded by hungry lions we see more clearly as metaphor.

But the presence of poems within the liturgy is only one way in which liturgy is poetry. Liturgical language is itself poetry. The vocabulary and the grammar of worship have at their root the multivalence and ambiguity with which our age seems uneasy. "Lift up your hearts," we have said for eighteen hundred years. Remember in the 1960s when liturgies tried to "contemporize" that line into some one thing the line meant? The metaphor is more than its translation, and it allows for a kind of communication different from that of the classroom teacher calling the children to attention. When we call the church, or God, our nurturing mother; when we call the pope, or God, our Holy Father; when we say we are washed into a family which dines on Christ's body at God's table: we are using metaphoric language. Some of these metaphors—God as Father—are so essential to our communication that they are creedal, determinative of our Christian identity. Others—God as mother—are uncommon and so still retain the metaphoric quality of surprise.

An example of the poetry that is liturgical language is the Exultet, the Easter Proclamation at the Vigil. Here in the middle of the dark night a single burning candle is lauded as the greatest light the world has ever seen. Rather than talk about Christ and the resurrection, the chant sings of the light and the night. The light is "the splendor of the eternal King," and it shines brilliantly throughout the world enrobing the church in its fire. ("This one candle?!" "Well, no, Christ." "Well, why not sing to Christ instead of to the candle?" 'Well, because. Besides, it's not to the candle.") The candle is an icon before us, becoming other than it is, receiving us other than we are, as the chant transforms words into other than they appear. On this Saturday night the debt of Adam is paid back, Egypt's first-born are slain, Israel crosses the Red Sea, sinners are liberated from prison, hell is harrowed, and earth and heaven are married. The tragedy of Eden is called a "happy fault." In perhaps the most dizzy collage of images, the morning star arises from the grave to find one single candle burning, vanquishing night and itself becoming a beacon of light. Where our recently purchased paschal candle stops and where Christ takes over, it is impossible to say. Meanwhile the deacon is straining her eyes in the dark church to see the words of the chant, words which exult over the spectacular brilliance of the room!—one way to say that Christ gives life out of death.

Not only the language, but also the symbols of our liturgical experience are metaphors. We call the water of baptism, whether three drops or a bathful, a flood that drowns and a fountain that washes. It is both a womb of birth and the tomb of death. There is in our use of water in baptism the poem's inconsistency, rather than the logical extension found in discursive philosophy. We believe that baptism drowns, like Noah's flood and the Red Sea; yet in these stories God's people, far from drowning by water, escape the wet grave. So also with the meal. This bread and wine is the Last Supper, the meal at Emmaus, the body of Christ, the eschatological banquet, the food shared with Moses and the elders on the mountain of God. We are the body of Christ, sharing in the body of Christ, sharing the body of Christ. It is hardly surprising that our theological explanations of the sacraments are inadequate to the metaphors of the liturgical experience. The community of faith demonstrates through its liturgical life its participation in a reality too complex for discursive description.

The veneration of Mary is another example of the liturgy as poetry. Theological positions about Mary have not fared very well. On the one hand we have her bodily assumption, and on the other hand we have Christians so afraid of her power that they will commemorate any saint but Mary, thank you. Mary is the church's best symbol of grace, of the interaction between God and God's chosen people. The human bears the divine so that the divine can sanctify the human. The maid of Nazareth is the Queen of Heaven is the maid of Nazareth, and, as in all metaphor, it is the ambiguity of the paradox which makes the truth. Neither part is true alone.

But it is not only certain aspects of liturgy which are poetry. Rather it is the rite as a whole which is an extended poem. We need not be surprised when social anthropologists tell us that ritual action is metaphor. We need only to read in the domes of eastern churches, "Standing in the temple of his glory, we think we stand in heaven." The liturgy as a whole is a metaphor, a model, if you will, of the reign of God, where God's people assemble around God's face (is it a throne or a table we see?) to praise and to be signed and to feast. Most descriptions of the liturgy—whether as a family meal, a royal court, a tribal ritual, a classroom, a football game, a cosmic battle, or a concert hall— err in the first place because they are too simplistic. Only when all the paradoxes are juxtaposed—the fast and the feast, the

Hebrew synagogue and the marriage supper of the Lamb—can the rite become all it might be. For this reason John's triumphant Jesus is declaimed on Good Friday.

Some Implications of Liturgy as Poetry

It is easy to see in H.M. Muhlenberg's service order—the German liturgy used by Pennsylvania Lutherans in the eighteenth century—that those Christians thought of liturgy as theological prose. The liturgy is essentially a somewhat ponderous monologue delivered by the pastor. The spaces allowed for theological hymnody constitute the people's only significant contribution. For those Christians among whom the pastor was in large part the professor, the classroom overtones are unmistakable. In the same way, if we agree that liturgy is to be recognized as poetry, our liturgy will demonstrate the implications of this definition. We will now consider only a few of these implications as they touch the ministers, the participants, catechesis, and architecture.

It seems that in Anglo-Saxon times when a chieftan would gather his faithful warriors into his hall for a feast, a scop would chant tales of the heroic past while strumming time on a stringed instrument. Apparently these epic poems were not memorized, but composed anew each telling.

The scop is one image for the presider. The presider also has the outlines of the story, and the pattern of the liturgy is a recurring beat to give the chant its shape. Within that structure the presider works a weekly variation: lessons, sermon, prayers, and the great prayer. (Remember Justin's description of the eucharistic prayer? "The president then prays and gives thanks as well as he is able.") Through these the presider directs the people through the communal participation in the formative stories and actions of the past. The presider, like the scop, is a functioning poet, recreating anew each liturgy the old story of the cross and resurrection and its life in the church.

Other images are more commonly evoked to picture the presider. Some liturgists like best the image of the host graciously serving the meal. Found inside our regular vocabulary are images important to our understanding of the office. A *presider* is one chosen to chair an assembly; a *pastor* is one who shepherds stupid sheep; a *priest* is one authorized by special purity to offer sacrifice to the gods; a *minister* serves, even meekly. The term *celebrant* suggests that the liturgical meal is some kind of party, while the term *preacher* suggests that the liturgical meal is quite beside the point. The word *father* is still a wholesome image, providing of course that its connotation be primarily that of parent, not of male, and that it stand complementary to, not antithetical to, the image of presider as mother.

Besides the ministers are the participants, who join into the action one of several ways. They can be overwhelmed by the experience and so be absorbed into the liturgy quite apart from their own consent. Perhaps this is how small children are grabbed for several minutes at a time by music and movement to pay attention to liturgical action. Perhaps this is how a stunning cathedral liturgy will live in the memory for years. But in general, for St. Mary's Down the Block, this is not a desirable model. A better model than the captivated audience is the participating family, perhaps the Christmas reunion where everyone knows the family rituals and joins in the festivities freely.

Our recognizing liturgy as poetry has direct implications for catechesis. If the faith is about facts, then we line up the children and make them memorize catechetical questions and answers. (Well, it *used* to work!) But if we are dealing with poetry instead of prose, if we want the people incorporated into the liturgical life of the church, then we do not teach answers to questions. We memorize, not answers, but the chants of the ordinary; we explain liturgical action; we enlist people as lectors and assisting ministers; we design studies around the central images of Christian worship; we lead bible classes on the lectionary: that is, we immerse people into the constituent features of worship so that they, too, become part of the metaphoric exchange.

Those who design and renovate churches must think of the building as in some way a metaphor for the Christian religious gathering. Church architecture as liturgical poetry is a complex phenomenon. Just because the church is called an ark hardly suggests that we have recognized liturgy as poetry if we build our churches to resemble Noah's ark. Rather, the building, its construction materials, and its appointments, to say nothing of the ecclesiastical art inside and out, are part of the poem which is the liturgy.

A good exercise would be an investigation into one's own parish architecture, asking John Ciardi's question, "How does this poem mean?" English teachers ask of the metaphor of a poem, "Is it new, is it true?" That is, is the poem unique rather than imitative, and is it true, rather than inconsequential, petty, false. If we could possibly do otherwise, we would not hang a paper reproduction of da Vinci's Last Supper in our chancels. Nor would we fill up the chancel with plastic palms. There is something completely unambiguous about plastic flowers. They are always perfectly arranged, inexpensive, never wilting, never dying. But the metaphors in worship are always ambiguous, the things of the earth caught up into the things divine. Plastic flowers? rather, to image the cross, a small tree, potted plants, or flowers that both bloom and die. No small part of the liturgy is unambiguous discursive fact. All is part of the dance. As Wilhelm Loehe, a nineteenth century Bavarian Lutheran pastor, wrote,

> Just as the stars revolve around the sun, so does the congregation in its service, full of loveliness and dignity, revolve around its Lord. In holy, childlike innocence which only a child's innocent heart understands properly, the multitude of redeemed, sanctified children of God dances in worship around the Father and the Lamb, and the Spirit of the Lord of lords guides their steps.

But. But. Perhaps no discussion of the Christian faith and its liturgy can conclude without the But, the Christian rejoinder to all this human talk about poetry and metaphor and real flowers. None of this matters, none of it, unless we know that, indeed, none of it *does* matter, that even the most real flowers are not sufficient offering to God. We in our attempt to understand the liturgy and so perhaps to improve it, with our joyful effort to offer thanksgiving, we with the disciples too hastily flee from the vigil at the foot of the cross. God is in our meager—or magnificent—liturgies only because God was first on the cross, and only when we realize that we can do nothing but kneel at the cross is there any use in talking about kneeling as metaphor or about liturgy as poetry to God.

15

The Language of Eucharistic Praying

DURING THE FRENETIC YEARS OF LITURGICAL REVISION, FEW OF US had occasion for sustained reflection on the massive task at hand: rendering in contemporary American English the historic liturgy of our church. Those who were translating new Latin texts and those who were revising and redesigning their rites met in common pursuit of that modern language which best expresses the church's orthodoxy. In most cases, the translators and revisers were offering gratis their spare time to navigate through unknown waters. There were no channels, no buoys: it had been four hundred years since the Reformers had made a similar attempt, and such a complete revision of Christian rites has never occurred. It was not clear who should be at the helm: theologians, church historians, liturgists, bishops, English teachers, or poets. And when the storms came, and they did come, we did not know whom or what to throw over to appease the sea's anger. Indeed, because there had been little sustained reflection on the task, we found it difficult to defend our position. There was the further confusion caused by experts in somewhat related fields—professors of seventeenth century British poetry, perhaps—who disagreed at many turns along our way.

We now have occasion for the reflection which was difficult midstream. There is much to study: the texts of official revisions as published by every major Christian denomination in North America in the last two decades; published collections of liturgical materials; file cabinets filled with occasional liturgies. There are minutes from the committees whose liturgical dreams were never realized, as well as several significant committee reports setting down preliminary observations concerning liturgical language. Yet one hopes for more than simply a clinical report, fetal monitoring of the birth or an autopsy of the corpse, whichever you will. It is time not merely for description of two decades of liturgical revision, but for liturgical prescription: what is liturgical language? What are its constituent elements? How is it defined in distinction from religious language, conversational prose, and poetry? It is not merely the computer in us that desires clarification. We in the church worship God, and much of our praise and supplication is verbally expressed. We who say "our" God, not only "my" God, are obligated to converse with one another on the type and meaning of the words we use in common. Words are not peripheral. As a vehicle for communal prayer, words carry the incarnation and shape our consciousness—as well as the consciousness of our children to whom we pass on the faith.

Liturgical scholars are making a beginning at prescription by studying the language of eucharistic praying.[1] The eucharistic prayer is the liturgy in miniature, the sign of the entire rite. As the verbal focus of the liturgy, the eucharistic prayer contains the most concentrated prose of the liturgy. While the whole of Christian liturgy requires our sustained reflection, the eucharistic prayer itself is a logical place to begin—granting we remember that not even during the eucharistic prayer are words the only data we might consider. There are the tone, gesture, and person of the presider, the stance of the worshipers, the feel of the room—all of which would require a book to discuss. We begin, as have others, with the language of eucharistic praying.

The task has been to pray to the Judeo-Christian God in contemporary American English. Some have vociferously maintained that this is impossible, contemporary American English being too common or too ugly or too pagan for Christian prayer. But the preservation of Cranmerian English for liturgical purposes moves Christianity in a direction which logically rejects

1. Jean-Pierre Jossua, "Unofficial Eucharistic Prayers: An Appraisal," *Symbol and Art in Worship, Concilium* 132 (1980) 74–83; John Barry Ryan, *The Eucharistic Prayer: A Study in Contemporary Liturgy* (New York: Paulist 1974); Dennis Smolarski, *Eucharistia* (New York: Paulist 1982); Keith Watkins, "Eucharist, American Style," *Worship* 56 (1982) 401–411.

the incarnation by implying that God cannot become incarnate in the contemporary world. Christianity unlike Hinduism needs no Sanskrit to speak of divinity. We must hold the line at the few ancient nonvernacular terms we have—the LORD, Christ, Abba, hallelujah, hosanna, amen, eucharist, to name several—if we are serious that our God is God also of contemporary speakers of English.

Other voices pressed the question: what is contemporary American English? In a democracy where even a college degree does not insure a high or remotely uniform level of literacy, who is to judge which language is the most appropriate for prayer? It has been suggested that so diverse are our patterns of speech, listening to speeches of the last five United States presidents will demonstrate that the only linguistic indication of the educated, sophisticated American is a large vocabulary. Furthermore, liturgy is one of the few situations in which words are repeatedly, publically declaimed. How does this fact affect our choice of words, tone, and syntax? How does the biblical illiteracy of the contemporary world influence our use of historic imagery? We who cannot agree on so circumscribed a question as the meaning of the word "he" have a difficult task in prescribing liturgical language. This paper shall inquire into both logical positivism and the school of metaphor for possible assistance in liturgical prescription. The intent is not to legislate rigid rules with which to shackle future revision committees nor to discourage a renaissance of the ancient art of improvised prayer.[2] In fact, let us say it this way: we must agree on some linguistic prescriptions before we can know what we pray and before we can hope to reintroduce the freedom of extemporaneous eucharistic praying.

One way that the twentieth century has viewed language is through the categories of logical positivism, the British philosophical inquiry into the meaning of language. This mathematical model for language sees words as signs for specific exterior reality. Radical positivists find all religious utterance to be nonsensical because precisely defined referents cannot be agreed upon. But other positivists developed categories which believers could use in examining religious language. Adapting J.L. Aus-

2. See Allan Bouley, *From Freedom to Formula* (Washington, D.C.: The Catholic University of America 1981).

tin's categories, Donald Evans called the language of thanking, praising, and confessing "behabitive performative utterance": that is, prayers use language which expresses human behavior and which performs its intent in the saying of the words.[3] A.C. Thiselton and others have applied these categories to liturgy, but there is little consensus in their use of these terms.[4]

One can use Austin's categories in an analysis of the eucharistic prayer. Austin sees human utterance as being of different types: informative, cognitive, cohesive, performative and causative, and expressive and evocative. The eucharistic prayer is not essentially informative utterance, for its purpose is not primarily to point to and to name. Nor is it essentially cognitive; for while systematicians remind us of the necessary relationship between liturgy and doctrine, liturgy is not essentially theology, that is, cognitive writing about the nature of God, the incarnation, and the life of the church. A believer would deny that the eucharistic prayer is essentially cohesive, that is, socially necessary noises which promote human interaction regardless of the literal content of the phrases. Christian liturgy is not like the singing of a nonsense song over beer and pretzels.

The first section of an Antiochene anaphora can be summarized "We bless God." This is performative utterance. The event is performed by the speaking of the words. The meaning of the words, which is the praising of God, is effected as we thank God for creation and salvation. So also with the second section. In that the Verba function as part of anamnesis, our saying "We remember Christ" is performative utterance. Christ is brought to remembrance within the community by the words. However, the Verba function also as a plea that God remember Christ and so look upon us with acceptance. Thus the Verba are also our supplication to God, "Remember Christ!" as we express our faith in the cross and evoke the action of God upon the worshiping community. Supplication, then, is expressive and evocative. The third section, "Send the Spirit!", is also expressive and evocative utterance. In determining that prayer is performative and ex-

3. Donald Evans, *Logic of Self-Involvement* (New York: Herder and Herder 1969) 38.

4. A.C. Thiselton, *Language, Liturgy, and Meaning,* Grove Liturgical Study no. 2 (Bramcote, Nottinghamshire 1975). For contrast see works of P. Donovan, G.S. Caird, A. Jeffner, and R. Jenson.

pressive, we mean that the words are not adiaphora, accompaniment, a catchall for attitudes and opinions about God or the eucharist or the church. Because the language is performative and expressive, we are responsible for the precision of that language.

All that said, we ask: so what? These categories do not lead very far. Few liturgical specifics come from our conversation with logical positivism. The first chapter of Northrop Frye's *The Great Code* with its helpful analysis of the history of language suggests why positivism offers so little to liturgists.[5] Using Vico's schema for successive epochs in world history, Frye describes three major linguistic epochs: (1) the mythic, the age of the gods, in which language as metaphor is known as magical power, the primary mode being poetry; (2) the heroic, the age of the aristocracy, in which language used in typology denotes linear order, the primary mode being allegory; and (3) the democratic, the age of the people, in which language used as description corresponds to exterior reality, the primary mode being realistic narrative. For examples Frye cites Homer as type one, Dante as type two, and Locke as type three. Biblical language, Frye suggests, is a hybrid made of types one and two: language as word, as in Genesis and John, and language as allegory, as in Revelation. Thus the roots of liturgical language arise from uses of language no longer dominant in western philosophical and scientific thought. The questions of logical positivism arise because we live in the third epoch, in which language is to correspond in some definitive way to a factual exterior reality. It is not surprising, then, that when we take questions which arise in the third epoch and address them to language of epochs one and two, our answers are dead ends. Liturgical language is metaphorical and allegorical: it is not descriptive in the way that scientific thought has understood description.

Christian liturgy does not speak language in the way that Locke and his world speak language. We call on God, we name bread and wine body and blood, we pray for mercy, without finding it necessary literally to point to the realities of which we speak. Thus our wish to pray in contemporary American English

5. Northrop Frye, *The Great Code: The Bible and Literature* (New York: Harcourt Brace Jovanovich 1982) 3–30.

does not imply that we wish also to understand our language as Locke and Austin would hope. We ought not expect scientific analysis to give us much assistance. However, we maintain, along with Frye, that the language of epochs one and two is alive and well, simultaneous to the speech of the modern world. Far from being passé, metaphor and allegory are returning to favor, not only when "realistic" novelists like Doris Lessing and Bernard Malamud publish bizarre fantasies, but also when physicists publically admit to the metaphoric nature of scientific theory. It is as though the Holocaust we lament and the holocaust we dread have discredited a mental notion that language can contain reality. Thus to pray to the Judeo-Christian God in contemporary American English is to speak in ancient ways with contemporary language.

A second way in which the twentieth century has viewed language is with the poet's eyes. Words are seen not as mathematical signs but as metaphoric symbols.[6] It is as if these students of symbolic expression followed Carl Jung who began as a psychiatrist and ended a mystic. Philip Wheelwright's principles of expressive language—iconic signification, plurisignation, soft focus, contextualism, paralogical dimensionality, assertorial tone, paradox, and significant mystery—show how differently these critics talk from their logical positivist colleagues.[7] We might call these critics a school of metaphor, which has contributed significantly to recent philosophies of religious language. Ian Ramsey's discussion of models and qualifiers relies on an understanding of religious language as metaphor.[8] Wolfhart Pannenberg writes of the use of analogy in praise;[9] Edward Schillebeeckx acknowledges that religious experience uses linguistic models if only to break them.[10] Recent study of

6. See, for example, Ernst Cassirer, Language and Myth (New York: Dover 1953); Suzanne Langer, Philosophy in a New Key (New York: Mentor 1942); and Max Black, Models and Metaphors (Ithaca, New York: Cornell 1962).

7. Philip Wheelwright, The Burning Fountain (Bloomington, Indiana: University of Indiana 1962) 76–101.

8. Ian Ramsey, Religious Language (New York: Macmillan 1963). See works of Thomas Fawcett, John Macquarrie, Paul Ricoeur.

9. Wolfhart Pannenberg, "Analogy and Doxology," Basic Questions in Theology, tr. George H. Kehm (Philadelphia: Fortress 1972) 1, 215.

10. Edward Schillebeeckx, Interim Report on the Books Jesus and Christ (New York: Crossroad 1981) 24.

proclamation and parable relies on metaphoric analysis.[11] Some liturgical scholars have applied the techniques of metaphor to their analyses of liturgy.[12] Yet the metaphoric analysis has not become focused enough to provide much assistance. Furthermore some have written in an exaggerated fashion claiming liturgy to be poetry, which is neither true nor helpful.

It is not merely that literary critiques steeped in the language of metaphor might be tangentially interesting to liturgists nor that some of our number are newly fascinated with the early church's mystagogy. It is rather that the language of the Christian faith is grounded in a system of metaphor derived from the Hebraic religious experience. That we are created into a royal people; that a messiah is coming; that the Lord is resurrected; that God's Spirit has breathed on us: these Christian assertions are rooted in ancient Hebraic images of God as One and of the final vindication of the just. The original religious experience was expressed in a Semitic image; translated into Greek and later into the many languages of the Christian tradition, it was reinterpreted in light of the Easter events. If we had recalled the Ravenna mosaics of the sacrifices of Abel, Abraham, and Melchisedek, we should not be surprised that even our sacrosanct word "sacrifice" was originally a metaphoric term.

Christianity requires metaphoric thinking. We share with other religions the religious exercises: liturgical action, private devotion, pious deeds. Yet even these religious experiences are understood as metaphors for a religious sensibility which is not essential for God's salvation. God's grace makes ultimately unnecessary our religious exercises. The story of the repentant thief makes even our most devout liturgies only metaphors for our reception of grace. Furthermore, our key liturgical terms—priest, sacrifice, family, meal—are metaphors for realities which are more, perhaps even other, than the words claim them to be.

The eucharistic prayer itself functions as a great metaphor. A contemplative chooses the metaphor of silence to contain the meeting with God. Church musicians laud the ability of music

11. See, for example, Amos Wilder, *Theopoetic* (Philadelphia: Fortress 1976) and Sally McFague, *Metaphorical Thinking* (Fortress 1982).

12. See, for example, Romano Guardini, *Sacred Signs* (Wilmington, Delaware: Glazier 1979) and Balthasar Fischer, *Signs, Words and Gestures* (New York: Pueblo 1981).

to be an excellent metaphor for praise. Architectural styles offer diverse metaphors for the liturgical experience: the royal court of the Gothic cathedral, the family meal of the chapel in the round, or the assembly room of a Reformed congregation are different metaphors for our meeting with God. In the eucharistic prayer we depict the meeting of God with God's people by means of a table blessing become ritual sacrifice become communal affirmation and supplication. In corporate action one presider prays for the many, and the words of the prayer call for the action of God. This basic metaphor—eucharistic praying as worship of God—can be realized in vastly different ways, depending on the words used in naming God, the elements, and the people; on the images which overflow the text; on the syntax and tone of the sentences; and on the structure of the prayer itself. To investigate these elements of style is to make a beginning at liturgical prescription.

The first line of inquiry concerns the words of the text. How are God, the worshipers, the eucharist and its elements named? Must the language be traditional? How much variety and innovation are possible in word choice and juxtaposition?

Some literary philosophers, theorizing that human language originated in symbolic thought, refer to all language as symbol or image or metaphor. While they are philosophically and anthropologically astute, such usage muddies conversation concerning the distinctions within language. Yes, "woman" was a metaphor, derived from "wife-man," but for most people the metaphor has become a common name, its metaphoric connotations dead. Yet the words lady, gal, or dame comment metaphorically on the common noun woman. Similarly, father language for God was originally metaphoric. However, it is by ancient Christian tradition so much the primary metaphor as to have been accepted as a common name for God. Sometimes for better, sometimes for worse, the poetic surprise of the metaphor has been forgotten by the time the metaphor is tamed into an accepted and official name.

The eucharistic prayer employs just such acceptable words. In the West it has been called the canon, the compilation of acceptable terminology, metaphors approved by the ages and images tamed into the vernacular of Christian orthodoxy. Private prayer does not share the linguistic restrictions of the public liturgy. It is these restrictions which limit the liturgy's use of mystical prayer. For the liturgical text must be the meeting ground for the faith of many, so that to be the church is to pray this prayer. The experimentations of the last decades have shown that while one hopes that the drafters of liturgical texts have had their various consciousnesses raised, the ordinary of the liturgy is not to be radically oriented toward such consciousness raising, especially on a controversial issue of the moment. Yet this is not to consign the eucharistic prayer to boring vocabulary. We treasure the riches of the core vocabulary of the Christian tradition, and if our preaching, our catechesis, and our liturgical art were none other than explication of the vocabulary of our eucharistic prayers, we would have sufficient wealth to sustain us lifelong.

In a time of diverse biblical translations and accelerating biblical scholarship, it is not self-evident which are the sacred words. Far from a universal recognition that certain words are the sacred words, perhaps even too sacred to pronounce, we contemporary Christians do not agree on whether the tetragrammaton is appropriate to our liturgical prayer, whether "the LORD" is a culturally conditioned title, or how "Abba" should be translated. Recent inclusive language lectionaries are struggling with the terms Son of God and Son of Man. When we confront Frank Henderson's prolific research into the naming of God in postconciliar prayer, which demonstrates that "Father" has to a great degree replaced "God" as the name of divine address, apparently solely for the sake of euphony, we must question whether we know what we are about.[13] Thus while we strive for eucharistic prayers in which the words are those of the historic faith, we must admit that in a religion of translation and rapidly changing cultural matrices, even simple words are not what they seem.

Outside the small set of acceptable words lies a larger set of terms which while still theologically correct raise an eyebrow or two. Sometimes this language, slightly off center, is demonstrative of only one Christian tradition. In the *Lutheran Book of Worship* the translator of Hippolytus was obliged to render *offerimus* as "we lift before you," because of the idiosyncratically Lutheran refusal to use the verb "to offer" for the eucharist. In the Roman Prayer III a wondrously ambiguous petition introduces the name

13. Voluminous unpublished data.

"the Victim": even as ambiguity this would not be acceptable in many Protestant circles. There is a characteristically Methodist phrase in *We Gather Together* when the anamnesis begins "We experience anew." Indeed, insofar as the words of the prayer become denominationally idiosyncratic, just so much have the prayers become occasional as far as the entire Christian community is concerned. Denominational prayers are at present a necessity, but our search for an ecumenical prayer is, after all, the search for Christian unity.

The Common Eucharistic Prayer gives us examples of the language of faith.[14] Here are no surprises in the naming of God. An echo of the Shema is in "You alone are God," and even the metaphoric names for God—fountain of life and source of all goodness—are time-hallowed. We the worshipers are described in classic terminology: we praise, we were created to serve, we disobeyed, we are in covenant, we celebrate the memorial, we recall, we proclaim, we offer. All is familiar language of faith. Even when we cannot agree what the language means—as in our being formed "in your own image"—we do not contest the sacred quality of those English words. The elements of the eucharist are called bread of life and cup of salvation, holy gifts, the body and blood of your Son. The words appear in such position that those who still scrupulously require a moment of consecration find the language orthodox. Several long phrases are nearly direct biblical quotations: none will argue with "and that we might live no longer for ourselves but for him who died and rose for us." The abundance of words pointing to God's splendor and the Johannine description of the passion produce a sense of exhilaration which may be judged not wholly inclusive of the Christian mystery and not sufficiently aware of the pain of the world. But this is an error of omission, for there is little possible quarrel with the appropriateness of the sacred words which do comprise this eucharistic prayer.

For we have our sacred words. The sanctity of Christian religious language did not lie in its being Latin or Greek or seventeenth century English. The sanctity lies deeper than that, and our search for the vernacular does not imply that church talk is

14. Common Eucharistic Prayer, available in the *Book of Common Prayer* (1979) and in *We Gather Together*.

street talk. Although we may finally agree that certain branches we find in the ark of the covenant are not Aaron's rod but only dead twigs, that is not cause to toss out even the idea of the ark as a repository of holy things.

The second line of inquiry concerns the images in the text. What is the source of the images? Do the images arise largely or exclusively from the Bible? Which parts of the Scriptures are favored? Of the many nonbiblical sources from which images could arise—mythology, theology, hellenistic, continental, or contemporary philosophy, psychology, nature, personal experience, or the unconscious—only certain sources are appropriate inspirations for liturgical writing.

In general, biblical imagery is the foundation of Christian language. Orthodoxy is that body of theological and metaphoric speculation which explicates or at least complements the primary biblical images. In eucharistic texts synoptic and Pauline language is safer than Johannine, except for the characteristic line in which Christ embraces his passion: that is, we do not talk about the flesh of the Son of Man, and recent Aramaic studies have supported our tendency to drink the cup instead of the blood. Passover imagery has come to be balanced by temple imagery. Historical references to Israel and Jesus are preferred over poetic or apocalyptic images. Familiar imagery is safer than unfamiliar: a recent prayer which evoked Lady Wisdom was perhaps too esoteric for regular use. Mythological sources are useful only if they have long since been baptized into the tradition. Logos, an image from hellenistic philosophy, is acceptable: Jesus "the Christ," terminology from contemporary theology, is not. Since the natural world could as readily provide us with imagery of death as of life, the history of salvation becomes our main source for images of grace. One reason that a 1960s rendition of the Lord's Prayer which began "Our Father on the deepest level of reality" failed is that the Christian community does not define itself in pop psychological terms. Personal experience is perhaps the least appropriate source for liturgical imagery, for the community does not pray one another's private prayer. In even the most careful work by a single author, a personal viewpoint has shaped the imagery into an idiom which may be perilously exclusive. Perhaps this is why we have found poets to be poor drafters of liturgy and why our finest individual writers are sometimes improved by the rigors of committee revision.

A study of the churches' official eucharistic prayers shows that even ones which appear innovative have images arising almost exclusively from the Bible and from credally sanctioned philosophy. We look for example at Prayer C in the new *Book of Common Prayer*. The first line, "God of all power, Ruler of the universe," while not the classical *Domine, sancte Pater, omnipotens aeterne Deus*, is a direct adaptation of the language of Hebrew prayer, "O LORD our God, King of the universe." The acclamation about interstellar space, while reminiscent of gallactic maps in science fiction movies, is part of a listing which echoes the creation poem in Genesis I. It is indicative of our modern stance within creation that the prayer gives thanks for outer space—the world beyond ourselves, astrophysically—rather than for the land, as did Hebrew prayers, or for fellow creatures, as did the Genesis account. Rather than being the center of the universe, earth is a fragile island. But the statement that humankind "rules the creation" is once again completely biblical. The people's many acclamations, which heighten the sense of contemporary eucharistic praying, actually echo specific biblical passages. One image particularly denotes this prayer as an Episcopalian prayer; the petition which recalls the prayer of humble access appears largely to keep alive that famous image of the crumbs under the table. Yet even this is a biblically based image from the story of the Syro-Phoenician woman.

We do well to be reminded of Daniel Stevick's comments on the images of Christian liturgy.[15] He remarked that the Christian images, tending to be images through which the encounter between God and humankind is disclosed, are mostly transformational images tied to events of salvation history and linking the present worshipers with the continuity of the whole people of God. He also noted that unlike perfect metaphysical conceits liturgical texts mix metaphors freely so that several images per phrase could be explored in separate and diverse directions. One sees this mélange of imagery in the concluding paragraphs of this Prayer C: "Lord God of our Fathers; God of Abraham, Isaac, and Jacob; God and Father of our Lord Jesus Christ: Open our

15. Daniel Stevick, "The Language of Prayer," *Response* 16 (1976) 9.

eyes to see your hand at work in the world about us. Deliver us from the presumption of coming to this Table for solace only, and not for strength; for pardon only, and not for renewal." The opening invocation of the God of the Hebrew patriarchs demonstrates the dangers of liturgical innovation: ten years later we see this line as unfortunately sexist. At any rate, the Hebrew God is called on to transform old style Episcopalians into contemporary activists. In a response, Emmaus is offered as an image for the meal, in "Be known to us in the breaking of the Bread." The book of Hebrews lends to the concluding doxology the high priest imagery: and imagery it certainly is, for whatever Jesus of Nazareth was, he was not any high priest.

This wealth of images, juxtaposed and interacting, is what we recognize as healthy liturgy. For the liturgy is the corporate recital of the images of faith in praise of God: the shepherds hear the heralds, the demoniac screams "Holy One!" and we chant the Gloria; Isaiah's angels sing "Holy," the crowd yells "Hosanna," and I reverence the body; the bath kills, the death feeds, the sacrifice nurtures; the Lamb, slain for my festival, reigns forever; the maid of Nazareth is Mother of the Church and Queen of Heaven; and we, grubby lot, are kings and queens and priests. Together we recite the images, finding in them our history, our present identity, and our destiny. We pray these prayers in the same way as the early Christians painted simple and diverse drawings in the catacombs. This is perhaps what most liturgists would mean by "believing in the Bible": we claim its images as true for us.

Unfortunately it is true that a congregation of biblically illiterate people miss the imagery in even the most classic of eucharistic prayers. Abel, Abraham, and Melchizedek are hardly household terms. However, the requirement that eucharistic prayers resist imagery from non-Christian or private sources does not imply that every image must be immediately accessible to every worshiper. Even the simplest Christian image is paradoxical and bound to a history of faith and life; adequate expression of the faith is both subtle and complex. We are well to be rid of the primer prayers of the last few decades. Liturgy for children, for example, means liturgy in which explication and nurture are part of the total expression, so as to bring up the children into the pardoxes of faith. Children's liturgy must never mean liturgy which so oversimplifies faith and trivializes its imagery that Christian truth has been violated.

One of the everlasting tasks of liturgical educators is to explicate even the most common eucharistic imagery so its original religious truth shines forth. That bread is the body of Christ, that we are the body of Christ, that the meal is a sacrifice: it will keep us busy for years rekindling one another's astonishment at the religious truth of this imagery. Eucharistic imagery, even though it be traditional, must be presented with a brilliance and a force so that the life of the imagery again lives. To speak ancient imagery so that it is continually startling: that is a goal of eucharistic praying.

The third line of inquiry concerns syntax. While much of liturgical language is metaphoric, the liturgy becomes audibly understandable because the syntax is essentially discursive. We are a visual culture, unaccustomed to listening to formal speech. (Remember Augustine's amazement at first encountering a person reading silently to himself?) For a variety of reasons, among them Hitler and television, we have come to discredit high rhetorical style, and it is not self-evident how in contemporary American English we shape the sentences and form the sounds of liturgical language. Yet like in the ancient world when rhetoric was feared as potentially a vehicle of lies and so was made the core of the curriculum, so must we examine the syntax of liturgical speech.

Contemporary conservative Judaism nurtures a quite different child born of the same first century Hebrew parentage as our Christian eucharistic praying. Those Jews who pray in contemporary English evidence a style more like ecstatic utterance than the court petition which influenced early Latin prayer. Their sentences are loaded with successive appositive phrases; several long clauses are tied to another by commas; names, images, and attributes of God are piled on one after another. Note these characteristics in the following quotation from the Yozer: "Our King, our Rock, our Redeemer, Creator of celestial creatures, You shall be praised forever. You fashion angelic seraphim who await Your word beyond the heavens. In chorus they proclaim with awe the words of living God, eternal King. Beloved, pure and mighty are they, reverently doing the will of their Creator. In purity and holiness they raise their voices, singing praise and adoration. One to another they vow loyalty to His kingship; one to another they join to hallow their Creator. With clear, sweet tones they all sing in harmony, proclaiming, Holy, Holy, Holy is the Lord of hosts; the whole world is filled with His glory."[16]

But Latin Christianity leaned toward the West, and its adoption of the terse language of court petition is only one sign of its life under the emperor. Thus we Westerners have an ancient prejudice which judges succinct unambiguous clarity as the model for Christian corporate prayer. It would be interesting to challenge this prejudice. However much we are moved by black improvisatory prayer, mystical reverie, and charismatic intercession, most of us continue to use the rationalistic prose of the Roman court. Yet something of ecstasy has erupted in that great Christian prayer, the Exultet. Perhaps while more study is done on whether the pattern of Roman court petition ought remain the sole model for Christian eucharistic praying, even our regular eucharistic prayers can learn something from the ancient syntax of exultation.

Syntax includes two matters, the first being placement of words. Since the syntax is that of expository prose, there are to be no sentence fragments, no run-ons, no ungainly structures which confuse the ear. Some such concerns are minor: for example, to repeat the "to" in successive infinitive phrases assists the ear in hearing the English correctly. Other concerns are more essential. Formal English prose of a century ago with its balanced subordinate clauses and shapely participial phrases is considered archäic today. Fine English style today is quicker, simpler, without being sparse or simplistic. Yet formal expository prose is not colloquial speech, and the fact that most Americans do not often shape their language into corporate prayer does not mean that there is not a most appropriate way for that shaping when it is done. The reasoning behind the common judgment that collects can no longer include the descriptive "who" clause since we do not regularly address one another in that way is quite beside the point: corporate prayer might well be cast in a contemporarily stylized form of the language. (I think of the popularity of the recent etiquette book by Miss Manners, who maintains that just

16. *Mahzor for Rosh Hashanah and Yom Kippur: A Prayer Book for the Days of Awe*, ed. Rabbi Jules Harlow (New York: Rabbinical Assembly 1972) 115.

because the rules have changed, we are not to suppose that there
are no rules.)

One of the primary considerations of word placement is the
matter of tension. Contemporary poetry is high in tension. Metaphors are sharply juxtaposed, and in the tension is the poetic
truth. "April is the cruelest month" is an example of high tensive
language in which logical connections are replaced by abrupt
juxtapositions. The passiontide proper preface "that he, who by
a tree once overcame, might by a tree be overcome" contains
this high tension, and while some of us delight in that preface,
there are many clergy throughout the land who haven't figured
out who the "he" is. Writing with no tension is flat and dull.
Writing with too much tension makes auditory participation impossible. Liturgy, after all, is not poetry. Highly tensive language
belongs more appropriately in hymnody, where singers can ride
the waves and relish the whirlpools and where occasional
swampings are of less consequence than during the eucharistic
prayer.

We must ask how much space there is within the text. The
text is not to be too tight, but neither should there be too much
openness. One reason that Cranmer's collects appear to us
models of English writing is that Cranmer's expansion of Latin's
single words into English doublets provides just a perfect
amount of space within the prayer. The use of two synonymous
verbs illustrates that none of our verbs is wholly accurate, just
as *Domine, sancte Pater, omnipotens aeterne Deus* reminds us that
no single name is sufficient for our God. Yet if there is too much
space, the result is private reverie, for people's attention falls
through the cracks, which it ought not do in corporate prayer.

There is the question of tone. Perhaps we can most quickly
recognize what is the tone of eucharistic praying by hearing
the tone of what is not. John Barry Ryan's study of the famed
Oosterhuis table blessings rightly criticizes the tone of those
prayers.[17] In these prayers and in their countless popular
descendants, the tone of a single voice—quietly naming God,
finding identity, ruminating about the faith—is that of interior
monologue, a T.S. Eliot or William Carlos Williams turned presider. While we may feel comfortable with contemporary male

17. John Barry Ryan, *The Eucharistic Prayer*, 70–76.

monologue, it is an introspective whimper compared with the proclamation of the gospel and the cry for mercy in the rhetoric of the priest. Another example: while it is understandable that a campus community will compose a blues Mass, it is less clear that blues, a medium for private and usually sorrowful reverie, provides the appropriate tone for eucharistic worship.

The tone of eucharistic praying is one of gratitude to God, proclamation of the gospel, shared faith of the community, and plea for mercy. It is the tone of trust, not of doubt: if we are agnostics most of the time, we can believe at least during the liturgy. The tone assumes corporate prayer in the assembly: thus it cannot be too quiet and soft. Yet the presider is as well leading a meal prayer: thus the praying ought not be raucous. The words of our praying carry in their melody line the songs of the angels, and thus one cannot imagine a flip tone to be appropriate. Yet our exultation is born of a crucifixion. Perhaps Thomas calling out "My Lord and my God!" towards the wounds of Christ can inspire our tone. "Therefore let us offer to God acceptable worship, with reverence and with awe: for our God is a consuming fire."

Syntax also includes the sound of the words. ICEL's "Principles of Liturgical Translation" deals with rhythm, patterns of stress which cultivate congregational participation, Saxon word roots, alliteration, assonance, and repetition; John Foley deals with vowel patterns.[18] These are notoriously difficult matters to articulate. One thinks of Edgar Allan Poe's essay in which he described his composing the poem "The Raven": his scientific, labored defense of the poem's aural effects strikes us funny, and we do not know if he is teasing or not. ICEL offers good advice in the search for euphony, for our prayers must at least sound pleasing. Yet great prose always breaks the rules. Our search is for more than euphony. The transformation of euphony into participatory praise and prayer is more than the responsibility of the presider's voice, for even a fine speaker cannot bring forth genuine life from a sedating text. Some small thing of Gerard Manley Hopkins' "Because the Holy Ghost over the bent world broods with warm breast and with ah! bright wings," which

18. John Foley, "An Aural Basis for Oral Liturgical Prayer," *Worship* 56 (1982) 132–152.

breaks every rule of stress patterning, can accompany our linguistic understanding of weak and strong syllables.

For various reasons it is not uncommon for Roman Catholic presiders to choose one of the "eucharistic prayers for masses with children" as regular parish fare. While one can appreciate the Roman Catholic search for newer compositions, one would wish for prayers of a higher order, even (I say especially) for children. The opening of the first prayer for children is prosaic in sentence structure and relies on the gushy phrase "all the wonderful things" to raise the sentence from the street. The tone of simpleminded thanks—praise for daylight, no praise for the night—is not noble enough to recall the crucifixion, or the holocaust, or last week's nightmare. After the Sanctus the praise to the Father has flat sentences—"You are always thinking about your people"—with uninspired vocabulary and weak stresses. Prose like "He loved everyone and showed us how to be kind," "we want to show you that we are grateful," and "we do now what Jesus told us to do," which by the way would never win a children's book award, does not call either children or their attendant adults into the festival of faith, the exultation of the angels, or the human plea for mercy. Dull eucharistic praying is a kind of liturgical sin against the Holy Ghost, and children are more likely even than adults to suffer from our lazy writing. The syntax ought be splendid enough to command our delighted attention.

The fourth line of inquiry concerns structure. How much are we bound to the Antiochene structure? The question is not only whether we can prefer the Alexandrian or whether we could return to a primitive form of the prayer as a series of loosely connected petitions. We are asking whether there is a clear value in our maintaining as normative the classic western anaphora. What about all those experiments of the last two decades? What can or ought we adopt from obsolete or from other eastern patterns?

An ancient eucharistic prayer of classic structure in current use is the Hippolytus canon. Examining the translation offered in the *Lutheran Book of Worship*, we find the familiar pattern: praise to the Father for creation and redemption; recollection of the Supper, anamnesis and oblation; epiclesis; doxology and Amen. Yet even in this ancient example the familiar pattern has its unique qualities. Creation is Johannine; salvation history is told not with the historical details of the life of Israel or Jesus but with the mythological language of the conquering hero. The Verba are included not as consecratory formulae, but as the sign of the climax of salvation history, the Last Supper providing the historical context for the philosophical language of John and the mythological images of redemption. The oblation utilizes the temple metaphor for Christian worship. The position of the invocation of the Spirit recalls the Hebraic plea for the kingdom rather than medieval controversies about the moment of consecration.

This structure for eucharistic praying can be variously interpreted. Usually the Trinity or Hebrew table blessing is evoked. Don Saliers suggests a theological outline, thanksgiving following by supplication.[19] As to the position of the Verba, while a rigid interpretation of consecratory function is unpopular now, the central position of the Verba is a sign of the centrality of Christ in Christian prayer, for when we address God as Trinity, when we offer thanksgiving and supplication, it is because we plead Christ.

When questioning the value in maintaining an historic structure, certainly liturgists are biased in tradition's favor. As we pray the eucharistic prayer, we join with the saints of the ages who join with the song of the angels, and our identity in this lineage is no small thing. For so we wear ancient vestments and retain the classic order of the Mass. Perhaps our ancient prayers ought to be identified as such, so that everyone can join the liturgists in realizing how many centuries of Christians have prayed thus. For the present, then, let those who propose a different structure attempt their case. The innovations in structure which appeared over the last two decades did not commend themselves. The prayers which were essentially table blessings are efforts at repristination which ignored the fact that our eucharist is not solely a meal. Those which were shaped by a particular theology or set of images were narrow in their focus. The eucharistic prayer is itself a type of Christian worship, and a form centuries in use functions as an underground stream

19. Don Saliers, "Theology and Prayer: Some Conceptual Reminders," *Worship* 48 (1974) 230–235.

which like Hagar's well can surface as life-giving to our present thirst.

In conclusion let us affirm that in eucharistic praying there are boundaries to heed, that certain words, images, syntax, tone, and structure are more appropriate than others, while some are wholly ill-advised. But attention to these guidelines must be balanced with awe for the task at hand. Individual authors may produce prayers too idiosyncratic, or they may not; committees may edit prayers into lumpy pablum, or they may not. There is finally that element of composition most difficult to define—we are tempted to label it genius and be done with it—a something which has knelt before the burning bush, which has eaten and drunk with God and lived, which has touched the wounds of Christ, *and* which knows the rules of contemporary American English. It is said that musicians ought to give recitals only if they play so well that the audience is forced to listen. Have we such believing writers of prose whose skill with eucharistic praying can compel the worshiper to come in? Thomas Merton, in "Senescente Mundo," wrote of the eucharist:

> Yet in the middle of this murderous season
> Great Christ, my finger touch Thy wheat
> And hold Thee hidden in the compass of Thy paper sun.
> There is no war will not obey this cup of Blood,
> This wine in which I sink Thy words, in the anonymous dawn![20]

We can all agree that these are not the words, images, syntax, and structure for eucharistic praying. Perhaps such language could work in hymnody—although Thomas Aquinas' *pie pellicane* was carefully edited out of "Adoro Te" by Cardinal Newman! Yet a four year old girl, striking a fine orans position in her mother's gold bathrobe, declaimed this prayer:

> God, thank you for the love of God
> and for the community of the holy.
> For we eat of the bread and drink from the wine.
> Love is God.
> We are the community of the Holy Spirit

20. Thomas Merton, "Senescente Mundo," *The Tears of the Blind Lions* (New York: New Directions 1949) 32.

in all the harm and danger.
Amen.

This four year old already has joined us in unconscious knowledge of our common eucharistic language. Perhaps we as habitual drafters of new eucharistic prayers ought to emulate that four year old: she is faithful to the tradition, gently eloquent, and wholly unassuming.

16

Sin: One Image of Human Limitation

IT IS NOT SURPRISING THAT THE TWENTIETH CENTURY CHURCH FINDS itself confused concerning its use of the category "sins." Of course there has never been absolute consensus concerning this complex idea. What is sin to one person has not necessarily been sin to another. For example, the tradition of Christian pacifism illustrates a historic disagreement over the morality of national defense: we do not agree whether defensive warfare is sin. But contemporary confusion runs deeper than debates over whether specific acts are sins. Religion sees God answering the needs occasioned by human limits: because we are creatures, we need a god. In the West the dominant image for our creatureliness, the recurring model of human limitation, has been sin. But sin has not been the sole image for human need, and presently it is not the existentially operative image for many Christians. The intellectual question parallels the church's dilemma over confession. Do people, ought people, attend confession? Why, why not? But before we can address the pastoral implications of this issue, we must step back to examine the image sin and to consider alternate images for human limitation.

The task of western consciousness has been self-awareness before God. The plays of the Greeks, the writings of the philosophers, the poems of the prophets, the religious and cultural rituals of past civilizations, all attest to the same struggle: given the existence of God, we must come to know ourselves. Granting belief in a personal diety, the Westerner comes to self-knowledge. Even Don Quixote conceived of his mission as a service to God as he cried out in highest comic irony, "I know who I am!" Contemporary atheistic philosophy as well stands in the tradition of those whose language was developed within religious presuppositions. The repeated western answer to this quest has been that we come to know ourselves as limited before God who is limitless. That we are not God is the first level of philosophical inquiry, and the most common image used to label this limitation is sin. Linguistic sophistication teaches us how to trace the development of this our dominant model: Paul Ricoeur's *Symbolism of Evil* suggests one key to understanding the Judeo-Christian identification of evil with sin. The origin of the word sin in the literal verb "to miss the mark" reminds us of the metaphorical nature of this label for human limitation.

The literature of the ancient western world suggests that the earliest understanding of sin is actually closer to our word sins. That is, human beings committed specific immoral acts for which the deity holds them responsible, or they perpetuated specific antisocial actions which rendered them unclean before God and the community. Oedipus is searching to know who he is, and in true western fashion his discovery is not only who are his parents, but also that before God he is the guilty one. The people of Israel after the Exodus define themselves as those set free, and in this process of self-knowledge they receive the tables of the law. Theological reflection evolves the primitive list of specific infractions into the philosophical concept of sin. Sin becomes the dominant western language used to describe the reality of being human. Sin is the demonstrable separation of the human from the divine, a label for the distance between a limitless God and limited humankind.

In order to analyze the image sin, let us quickly trace its preeminence as a Christian category for human limitation. The God of the Hebrews is described throughout the Old Testament as a God of judgment and mercy. This implies a people who sin and need forgiveness. One aspect of the Garden of Eden story is that Eve and Adam are guilty of sin. The prophetic literature calls the people to self-consciousness over sins—specific examples of idolatry, selfishness, and injustice—and over sin—the terrifying distance from a saving God. The gospels interweave narratives of the life of Jesus with the interpretation that what Jesus did was to forgive sin. In Mark 2 the miracle of the healing of the paralytic is made a sign of the essential task of God's forgiving sins. The tradition of western theology has been shaped to great degree by what we might call "male mid-life crisis theologians": Paul, Augustine, Luther. Like Dante in the first stanza of *The Inferno*, these men were wandering in mid-life and discovered that their search for God and for peace in truth was impeded by the human limitation they identified as sin. Anselm's theory of atonement which exercised enormous influence over theology and liturgical practice also conceived of the great human problem, distance from God, as being occasioned by sin and of the church as the agent of a forgiving judge, meting out forgiveness of sins. Still today acts of confession are a pastoral application of this image. The faithful are guilty of sin which must be forgiven before the joy of divine life can be celebrated.

Do we confess sin or sins? The confusion between these two words is no small matter. "To confess sin" is to acknowledge one's distance from God, to declare oneself human before God. To confess sin, like to confess the creed, is to state self-awareness. But "to confess sins" has come to mean a groveling under guilt, a listing of infractions, a laundry list of what must be cleansed before one can come to the table. Theologians hope to teach that the greatest human limitation is sin, that sin is the fact of distance from God, and that God bridges this distance with mercy. Yet catechesis continues to define sin as observed in sinful acts. Not the great prophets of Israel nor contemporary preaching has succeeded in describing sin other than by evoking lists of sins. In the penitential rite of the American Roman Mass, we the faithful "acknowledge our failures," "ask the Father's forgiveness," and "call to mind our sin." In the Simple Rite of Adult Initiation, the litany before the exorcism contains eight petitions, six of which are specifically about sin and the remaining two which imply it. Thus the faithful, in order to meditate upon their human limits, are asked to recall infractions of God's law. The current practice of abstracting sins implied in the Sunday lessons and so composing the petitions of a penitential kyrie is another example of human limitation being construed as sin because of sins. All this occurs, by the way, with little or no attempt to contrast the Torah with Paul's radical Christian ethic in Galatians.

Perhaps this worked better in a simpler age. People went to confession both because they respected church authority in a more literal manner than at present and because having been catechized on a single set of morals, they genuinely felt guilty over infractions and sought release from their guilty conscience through forgiveness of their sins. Now that we know a good deal about the history of ethics and are aware of diverse ethical systems, it is nearly impossible for a group of contemporary people to agree on absolute moral positions. The current Christian debates over the nature and moral implications of homosexuality or of abortion demonstrate the monumental disagreements coexisting in contemporary Christian ethics. Some of the most thoughtful Christian ethicists are the ones least sure of moral absolutes.

To the extent that sin has become identified with a list of sins, and to the extent that I can receive opposite pastoral counsel as to whether a specific human act is a sin, I will not know whether to confess to God. If I feel guilty, I will not know whether that is my mother's voice nagging me or God's word speaking to me. If I do not feel guilty, I probably do not judge myself guilty, and will not confess. I cannot trust my feelings of guilt or of freedom; I cannot evaluate moral behavior before God and the community. Our time is a moral free-for-all. The Holocaust is not the exception but the paradigm of a century of moral anarchy. There is no longer in the culture or in the church a relatively undisputed moral authority. For example, a growing number of Christians believe that couples living together before marriage is a healthy social experiment parallel to first vows in monastic life. What do we say? Is this phenomenon an instance of rank immorality, or is it a cultural adaptation of courting rituals which, like any human behavior pattern, can serve us either toward good or ill? It is ironic that while the western search for self-awareness developed in tandem with a high consciousness of sin, that search has brought us to a time of acute self-awareness yet a diminished, if not nonexistent, consensus about sin.

However, sin is not the only western Christian image of human limitation, and this fact must inform our panic over the confusion with sin and sins. One alternate image for human limitation is mortality. Like sin, mortality has its own history of use in the tradition. God is God because God creates life and has life forever, and human limitation is manifested in that we must die. The Genesis story says that the angel guards the tree of life from Adam and Eve so that they may not eat and live forever, and the Scriptures' move toward the Apocalypse brings the faithful back to the tree of life, that they may finally eat and live. The covenant with Noah is a promise for life against death. The hope of the patriarchs for a son is a hope for life in the face of death. Abraham was not concerned about sin and forgiveness: he wanted a son before he died. One interpretation of the incarnation is that God by living and dying as a human being alters our despair over death. By joining us in death, God gives life to death. The resurrection of Jesus is a literal response to our primordial terror of death: we too like Christ will live again. It is true that Christian theology has often interpreted the meaning of the resurrection as the forgiveness of sins. But in the first place, prior to interpretation, the resurrection as an image is part of a complex about life and death, eternal life conquering death, a new life after death. John 3 uses the image of our being born again to new life. The orthodox emphasis on deification develops this image: God became human so that we can become divine, thereby conquering mortality. The Paschal Vigil is based on the image of life conquering death, and its repeated reference to baptism is not about forgiveness of sin but new life. Current experiments in feminine imagery for God develop the image of death and birth to life, the crucifixion not as forgiveness of sins but as the labor pains toward new life.

A third significant image for human limitation throughout the tradition has been injustice. In the narrative of the Exodus, evil was the outside oppressor, and God was the liberator. The title of messiah reflects this metaphor, for in the reign of the anointed one the just would be vindicated and external evil overcome. This image is especially corporate, for God will save a whole people from all its outside enemies. Apocalyticism exemplifies this image: the anti-Christ is out there in the world, and hope for the future lies not in self-criticism or in resurrection but in liberation from those evil regimes. The woman in Revelation 12 is bearing the personification of justice into an evil world. In that the primitive church speculated whether or how much one sinned after baptism, this image was the operative model. Liberation theologies rely on this language: radical Marxist, black, and feminist theologies see the greatest human limitation in the systemic evil of which the inside group is relatively innocent and against which the freed faithful are rallied in order to spread God's liberation. Baptism which grants Christian freedom is thus pictured as an anointing to overcome injustice in the world. The intercessions in the eucharistic liturgy demonstrate the whole church's belief that God has the power to effect justice in the world and so demonstrate divine dominion. The Jehovah's Witnesses are a sect for which this image of injustice has become essential.

There are obvious pastoral problems in designing rituals for a church in which some people resonate to the sin/forgiveness image and others to the injustice/justice image. The sin/forgiveness image urges self-criticism and constructs litanies of self-evaluation. It cultivates and even requires the self-reflective consciousness. (Thus arose the notion that children must be of the age of moral consciousness before they can commune.) However, those who live by the injustice/justice language see this first group as comfortably religious, contented to play out a ritual game of confession and forgiveness while ignoring the massive problems of the poor and the oppressed. The passion of liberation theologies to free society's slaves cannot find assurance in self-contained interior monologues and ridicule this addiction to sorrow and obsessive flagellation. Yet those confessing their sin will judge the liberators as in their own way comfortably self-serving, easily excusing themselves from sin. There will likely be in fact direct conflict in which an action labeled sin by the first group will be lauded as liberation by the second. Yet the two images must stand in tension. Even in the Scriptures these two images coexist. When the one who forgives sins is named messiah, forgiveness and liberation have met in Christ.

A fourth image for human limitation is disease. This image tends to be used in a highly individualistic manner. The psalms which plead or praise for healing are cast in the first person singular. Although this image has not been prominent in mainline theology, we must admit that the majority of stories about Jesus are of a healer. The lepers are cleansed, the blind receive their sight. The etymology of the title Savior connotes physical healing. Faith healing has been periodically in the church a popular image of what salvation is, and miracles of healing have been lauded as signs of God's power in the saints. Because of the psychological movement, disease/wholeness has become an increasingly significant image in the twentieth century. Racks of paperback books, weekend retreats, services of healing, and a revival of the rites of anointing demonstrate this image of disease/wholeness in action. Henri Nouwen's enormous appeal attests to the resonance of this language in our time.

A fifth image for human limitation is meaninglessness. Before God ordered the universe there was *tohuwabohu*, meaningless chaos. The narratives which tell of the call of the prophets indicate a vision of life in which focus and meaning for human endeavor come from the word of God. Lady Wisdom expressed the Hebrew's hope for beauty and order in chaos. The title of Logos sees in Christ the answer to the human search for meaning: in Christ is word, divine reason, order, meaning. The story of the slaughter of the innocents places Christ within the chaos of human history not as a solution to this meaninglessness but as Emmanuel, God with us. In such a Christology, God becomes incarnate to join us in our meaningless existence and so accompany our struggle for purpose. In Mark's Gospel the only cry of Jesus on the cross is his agony of abandonment by God, and in John's Gospel, when Philip asks to see God in order to be satisfied, Jesus points to his own life among them. Many modern people are not obsessed by sin, afraid of death, overwhelmed by injustice, or racked by disease; but they are desperate for meaning. Christian existentialism offers a sophisticated expression of this image. We cannot be certain whether there is any absolute truth, any ultimate meaning, in life. Like Job, we are baffled by the suffering of the innocent, and we doubt the answers we have been led to believe. Within the chaos we join hands with those who believe in a God who in Christ joined us in human meaninglessness, who offers us a community with which to stride into the future in the faith of realized beauty and order at the end of time. How can we know that the meanings we assume do in fact obtain? Where is Logos in *tobuwabohu?* With this quest for meaning as the dominant image, liturgy is understood as ritual action which begins each week under the paradoxical sign of the cross by ordering chaos into beauty, hospitality, and faith.

No doubt there are yet other images for soteriology beyond these five: sin/forgiveness, death/life, injustice/justice, disease/ wholeness, chaos/meaning. We have already touched on some of the consequences of this variety of images. Let us quickly rehearse these implications: It is ignorant to act as if one of these systems is the only orthodox Christian system. It is myopic to maintain any one image to the absolute exclusion of the others. It is fruitless to attempt to offer a solution from one set to people who understand life under a different set. It is difficult to construct pastoral rituals which are mutually beneficial to people within different systems. It is likely that one's predilection for any one image is a result of one's life experience. It is tempting for any one image even when consciously and conscientiously maintained to become narrowly self-serving.

Awareness of the relative nature of the image of sin and forgiveness suggests to us many disturbing questions. Why has sin become the dominant western category for human limitation? Ought sin/forgiveness remain paramount? How much do theologians wish to grant partial or full legitimacy to one of the other images? Do the truths articulated by liberation and feminist theologies and the insights explored by psychology and philosophy warrant liturgical rituals in their own language? What is the relation of Christ to human limits as variously described? Which images of God correspond to each image of human need? Ought we try to maintain several or all of the images in order to benefit from the varied expression of truth? How do we individually or corporately profit by our favorite image? How many such systems can a person simultaneously maintain? What is the God beyond our chosen set of images? Which images can most clearly speak grace in our time? How can we train our preachers to ask these questions before they compose their sermons? Undoubtedly there are more questions: this is enough for now!

There is little integrity in urging contemporary people to confess their sin if we cannot defend our answers to at least some of these questions. In the Scriptures the images overlap in Christ, and our growing realization that the God of Christ must be bigger than the western self-reflective consciousness as articulated by the sin/forgiveness image must make us open to these and other images. We need articulated Christologies and explications of soteriology which develop these significant images for human existence upon which to base liturgical formulas. For the people need the images true enough to their experience and deep enough in the Christian tradition that they may have the foundational language upon which to base their lives. The confessional box may be vanishing, but we do not know what all to put in its place. Its replacement by a pleasantly appointed counseling office has not struggled fully with the complex depths of the problem.

In judging from among images for human limitation, there is yet another criterion. Knowing human limits ought to be a comfort. We learn from the transparent honesty of children, and we come to know in the critical decisions of adult life, that limits are good and wholesome gifts of truth. The railing on the crib, the rules of hopscotch, social etiquette, ethical restrictions, the embrace of the lover, the facts from the oncologist, the dirt on the coffin, are in fact limits which keep us from the anguish, forelornness, and despair of ultimate Sartrian freedom. Human creativity flourishes within bounds: we must then know those bounds. In ancient myth, humans who were granted eternal life always came to rue it: we welcome limits as a closure to license. We must then ask which images of human limitation do contemporary people hear with relief, even with joy. To which images do we say a sad and happy Amen, being turned by such a God from such a limitation with delight? Human limitation so articulated would be good news indeed, and we people would flock to hear the words embrace us in our need. The image must be such that it can convey transforming grace. For human life will not escape the limitations: our only hope is that God can transform us within those limits, and as W.H. Auden wrote, "In the prison of his days, teach the free man how to praise."

Finally there is gratitude for the diversity of images. Even in the Apostles' Creed the divine life of Christ in the Spirit is expressed in a variety of images: the holy catholic church, the communion of saints, the forgiveness of sins, the resurrection of the body, and life everlasting. Here God's Spirit is pictured as an ordering of human chaos, a model of justice in the world, our final return to wholeness, and the overcoming of death, as well as the forgiveness of sins. Christ is Forgiveness, Resurrection, Messiah, Savior, Logos. The task of the liturgist is to find the images which best proclaim the mystery of the gospel in the vernacular to a living people, and this endless endeavor requires of us the study of both the biblical and traditional Christian images and also the contemporary categories of human need. Perhaps the more images, the better.

NAMING GOD

17

Language about God:
Muddle and Mystery

ONE NEED NOT LOOK FAR OR DEEP INTO THE CHRISTIAN CHURCH
today to discover a muddle over the question of the naming of
God. Some conservative scholars uphold the biblical and traditional language as inviolate; some radical feminists demand thor-
ough-going change lest they follow Mary Daly out of the church;
pious Christians caught in the middle find it difficult to evaluate
the arguments. Partial answers avoid some of the hardest questions, and throughout the controversy it is hard to balance the
intellectual and learned theological leadership with the piety of
the people. The matter is, after all, an urgent one. Contemporary
Americans are aware of the sexism in much of the traditional
naming of God, and we are called to examine the connection
between this masculine bias and the western cultural dominance
of the male. But incomplete and superficial solutions can turn
well-meaning reformers into religious sectarians, and the muddle in the church as a whole remains.

Yet we cannot become overwhelmed by the muddle. *Always
in the Judeo-Christian tradition the name of God is mystery:* the fire
which does not burn the bush; the consonants which cannot be
pronounced; confession of Thomas to the risen Lord. Perhaps
we know best the philosophical tradition of theology which tries
to clarify articulately the nature of God and the meaning of God's
name. But throughout the Christian tradition are those who affirm the mystery of the name: the psalms with their barrage of
images; the Revelation with its incoherence of glory; the mystics

who found unique ways to describe their religious ecstasy; the musicians who rely on the music beyond words; and the contemplatives who are overwhelmed not by muddle but by mystery and in the end keep silence.

It is in reverence to this mystery that we seek to answer our current dilemma. The problem is complex enough and requires so much study and documentation that a short article cannot begin to be a final word. But in a few pages we can at least list the questions. Without attention to all the following issues, any answer we would offer is partial and irresponsible. We may of course address these concerns and still propose only meager solutions. But at least we will not have been irresponsible.

The Inadequacy of Language

The twentieth century philosophical tradition has examined language extensively, and in the main linguistic philosophy has probed the question of accuracy. That is, how do we know that the words we use are true? How do words correspond with reality? Greatly influenced by mathematics in which a mark on the page or a blip in the computer is a universally accepted sign for exterior reality, philosophy asks the same of language: that it be verifiable, that it be accurately a sign for reality, and that, in the interests of clear communication, we who use those words agree on their referent. When I say "cat," I am speaking of a real thing and all speakers of American English will know to what I refer. Do I mean only the domestic cat, or am I including the tiger when I say "cat"? Well, let us agree on meaning: then language will be true.

While this philosophical tradition of logical positivism is dominant today, it cannot be our model for religious language. *Human language cannot adequately name and describe God*, for that is the very gulf between human and divine. If we would wholly describe God, it would mean that our minds could embrace divinity and our language contain it. This is not merely nostalgia for an ancient understanding of language: it is belief in divinity, that is, in a level of reality beyond the level to which we have ready access. The Judeo-Christian tradition has always stressed this inadequacy of human language. Thomas Aquinas, after writing book after book of philosophical theology more definitive for a longer time than any other works in the tradition, had a vision of God and ceased writing altogether, saying, "All that I have written seems to me like so much straw compared to what I have seen and what has been revealed to me. (*Friar Thomas D'Aquino: His Life, Thought, and Work*, by James A. Wesihiepl, O.P., New York: Doubleday, 1974, p. 322.) The Hebrews did not pronounce God's name, and the Cistercians provide a haven for those who want their lives of silence to acclaim the unspeakable God.

Of course Christianity is not mainly a mystical religion. The Word became flesh: our God is a God who chooses to be born human and to speak through the prophets and apostles. Thus we are rightly held to a tradition of words to God and about God, a tradition which has shaped us and which in turn we shape. We must seek to reform our language and to make the words of our culture, which are different from those of the last generation, speak faithfully the mystery of God. But we cannot believe in the words themselves, as rigid dogmatists may like to do, as if the words really can express the essence of God. Always human words revolve somewhere around the divine center. When as a child I memorized that God is "eternal, unchangeable, omnipotent, omniscient, omnipresent, holy, just, faithful, benevolent, merciful, and gracious," it never occurred to me that, far from being descriptive terms like "red-haired," those adjectives are wholly inadequate words approximating our experience of meeting with God.

The Use of Metaphors

Thus the *first* questions to be asked: has the tradition acknowledged the inadequacy of its terms? Have the reformers acknowledged the inadequacy of their terms? What is our stance concerning the revelatory truth of our words? What is the relationship between revelatory truth and accuracy?

Because human language cannot discursively describe God accurately, we rely on images to approximate our vision of truth. Images are the pictures which we call to mind within the community, hoping that the forcefulness of the image will convey what explanations will not. The psalms most commonly evoke images of rock, fortress, and king in addressing God. These images were common words sanctified suddenly by being brought to speak of God.

It is important to remember that all images used in the names and descriptions of God are metaphors. A metaphor is an alien name: literary critics talk about metaphor as the tension produced by talking about two different things at the same time. The tension produced: the alien name does not naturally fit. We say that God is a rock. But we all know that God is not a rock. In this yes-no is the religious insight. How is God, who is most surely not a rock, the Rock? How is God, who is most certainly not a king, the King? We have been tricked into a dangerous religious naiveté when we forget that the image functions as metaphor, as something quite other. It is as if the rules of grammar and logic are superseded by the religious vision.

The Christian tradition is fraught with examples of the failure to remember what metaphor is. The centuries of oppressive male chauvinism which made fathers the head of the family and males the head of the church often looked to the metaphor as warrant for their action; they seemed to have forgotten that father-language for God and he-terminology for God function as metaphors. God is not a great father in the sky nor God a being of masculine sexuality, as these images suggest. For when images talk of God, they are always metaphors, always alien terms which surprisingly, astonishingly, get juxtaposed to God.

This is not to suggest that we toss out metaphors, condemning them as untrue. *Metaphors are all we have in speaking of God.* A religious tradition is a historic adherence to a set of metaphors: wholly to alter the metaphors would be to change the religion. Our task rather is to recall again and again for ourselves and one another the two different things that we are talking of at once. If we are struck dumb with awe before the Creator of the universe and the Artisan of the cell, then we are ready to wonder at Jesus' relationship with that God which inspires him to call God *Abba*. If we despair at the world order and bemoan the state of justice and peace, we can then pray to God as the king who rights wrong: yet even here we see that the metaphors are words of faith, for we can only hope that in the end time God will bring justice and peace, like a good king. The evidence now for our calling God a king is rather slim.

The Matter of Translation

Thus the *second* question to be asked: what metaphors can we use to express the mystery of our relationship with God? Are we careful in explicating our metaphors for their astonishing religious truth? What is our commitment to the metaphors our tradition has given us? How much is a religion adherence to a set of metaphors? Are we avid in finding new metaphors?

In some religions the words spoken by or about God are so holy that they cannot be translated into the vernacular. Sanskrit is still used as a religious language. Observing Jews learn Hebrew. But Christianity proclaims the incarnation, and in God's being born a human being we have our warrant for being what we have always been: a religion of translation. God is not back there in an ancient language; God is speakable in the vernacular. The disciples read Scripture in Hebrew and spoke in Aramaic; Paul wrote in Greek; theology was formulated in Greek and Latin; the Reformation preached in German, French, Dutch, English; and English and American Bibles and new books of worship continue to pour out of publishing houses. We Christians are free to clothe God with our vernacular; but with the freedom comes tremendous responsibility.

In the matter of God's name we can see the difficulty of translation. When Abraham meets God, the name of God is given as *El Shaddai*. Literally this means God of the mountains: it is an image of God's grandeur and mystery. *El Shaddai* is traditionally translated "almighty God." The power has been lost in translation, a vague adjective substituted for the vivid image. When Moses meets God, the vision is of a miraculous fire, and the name of God is given as YHWH, unpronounceable, untranslatable. The Hebrews in reading the sacred text read, instead, *Adonai*, Master. When Jesus prays to God, he uses the term *Abba*; and already Paul, writing in Greek, translated *Abba* as Father, instead of the more accurate Papa, my dear daddy. Thus while we rejoice in the immediacy of God which is granted us in a religion of translation, we have not even in ancient tradition a good track record on accurate translations.

The difficult matter is, of course, what constitutes translation. It is being suggested that *Kyrios* be rendered "the Sovereign One" and Son of Man "the Human One." While these may appear radical changes, they are still translations—and I believe fine

and responsible ones. Yet, while I admit that the matter of translation is not about individual words but about intellectual content, to add "and Mother" to biblical references of God as Father
strikes me as paraphrase, not translation. Indeed, some people
despair, arguing tht words spoken within an ancient philosophy
cannot be rendered within a different metaphysical universe.

Chauvinism in the Scriptures

Thus the *third* question: how are we to translate accurately
into contemporary American English what we claim is the word
of God?

It is no longer shocking to accuse the Scriptures of masculine
bias. In response to this accusation, some people claim that pa-
triarchy is the divine order and because of that, revelation reflects
it. Others view it as so offensive as to turn them away from the
tradition. Some feminist biblical scholars are helpful in showing
the feminism which does exist in Scripture and in postulating
feminism which was historically present but suppressed. But all
this fervor only demonstrates a growing consensus that the
Scriptures are written in a male-dominated culture, support this
male dominance in many ways, and find it natural to talk of God
in overwhelmingly masculine images. But there is, alas, no consensus about what stance we are to take before this chauvinism.
Are we to affirm it, translate it out, interpret it away, ignore it,
or reject it along with the gospel it carries?

Believers have been in similar situations before. Those who
oppose war must deal with a Hebrew tradition which saw the
people as a militarily aggressive nation. In the American south,
devout believers found it easy to support slavery with biblical
texts. Those who oppose homosexual behavior can cite biblical
passages in their defense. It is the age-old problem of herme-
neutics: what did the text say, and once translated and interpreted, what does that text say today? Is God called the King
merely because of the mythic pattern in the near eastern world
that the king is the son of God? Could we speak of God as Queen?

All Christian churches speak of the Bible as normative, but
they mean various things in saying that. Some repristinating
churches pretend that the application of the Scriptures in the
present is easy; but they too have a strong and solid tradition
of interpretation which mediates the "normative" Scriptures for

the church. The Protestant reformers, in discarding "tradition," were merely substituting their own younger tradition for one hundreds of years older. What we mean by normative will influence what we elect to do about the Bible's chauvinism, most sensitively in the naming of God. For there are plenty of gods around, and enough religions to enjoy some choice. But this religion called Christianity prays to *El Shaddai* YHWH *'Abba*, and the Sovereign One of the Pentateuch is the Sovereign One whom Thomas adores after the resurrection. It is this God, with these names, that we worship, preached by these Scriptures.

Thus some difficult questions are ours: what do we do with the Scripture's chauvinism? What mediating role can we as continuing tradition play interpreting and applying that Scripture to the present? How do we distinguish valid continuing revelation from irresponsible misinterpretation?

The Interpretation of Gender

In consideration of gender we see coming together considerations of language, metaphor, translation, and Scripture's normative character. Gender in many languages, including Hebrew, Aramaic, Greek, Latin, and German, is a grammatical category for nouns, pronouns, and adjectives. Grammatical gender has no meaning apart from its role as sentence organizer. A table is feminine, a chair masculine, and while some linguists postulate a prehistoric link between sexual tendencies and the object names, surely any such logical system has long been abandoned. No intelligent thinker in a language which has grammatical gender actually thinks of those objects as having sexual being or even sexual tendency.

In Hebrew, God is referred to as "he" because the word he is used, in Hebrew and in many languages until the mid-twentieth century, as the nongender-specific personal pronoun. In Hebrew, *ruah* ("spirit") is feminine because the noun *ruah* is a feminine noun, not, unfortunately for us, because they thought of God's spirit as a feminine being. While Hebrew poems play on *Hokmah* as God's Lady Wisdom, a kind of consort for God, when theologians speak seriously, they reject categorically any actual great woman in the sky.

The problem of gender is one particularly troublesome to contemporary Americans because American English has moved much farther much faster than even British English in replacing grammatical gender with natural gender. That is, increasingly for Americans, "he" means a creature of masculine sexuality. Dozens of linguistic adaptations and neologisms in the last decades demonstrate this move. Thus to Americans the concern is far more crucial than to speakers of French or German, for our saying God-he now implies masculine sexuality in God much more specifically than in the past when one might only sense a masculine bias.

The Meaning of Orthodoxy

Question: ought we, can we, in the next hundred years eliminate use of he for God? How do we read the Scriptures? Is it realistic to hope to retrain the entire church? Is America an anomaly or the vanguard?

It has become common recently to hear the Gnostic writings quoted as examples of Christianity with a more feminist cast. No one can dispute that these writings exist and that they have scholarly interest for the historian of religion and culture. But the Gnostic decision to use explicitly sexual terminology for God was rejected by the orthodox theologians of the church's early centuries. In fact, orthodoxy's responses to the Gnostics sound astonishingly applicable in some contemporary arguments in which the Spirit as feminine helps constitute a divine family. Now the question arises: what does it mean for us to remain orthodox Christians?

Some church members find the matter of orthodoxy an unhelpful shackle to the past. To them this matter is easily dealt with: they feel no need to remain orthodox. But to others the desire to remain in orthodox communion with the historic church is paramount, and for those this question must be addressed. Orthodoxy is the right practice of prayer: how do we pray? Who is our God? What do we ask for? In answering these questions of orthodoxy, one defines the religion. To be orthodox means to pray the right words in the right manner to the right God. Usually by orthodoxy we mean the historic tradition of reusing the same words. That is, successive generations of theologians may interpret the words in different ways, but they use the old words, the orthodox prayers. Those who do not adhere to the same words leave the tradition of orthodoxy.

Thus we must ask: *how much can we change the historic language of prayers yet remain orthodox?* What about the fact that some of the oldest ritual formulas—the Lord's Prayer and the trinitarian invocation—are precisely the places where father-language occurs? The opening line of classic eucharistic prayers always calls God Father: *Domine, sancte Pater, omnipotens aeterne Deus.* We must decide what in the tradition is the inviolate core. Certainly there is a great deal of the Christian tradition which is oppressively weighted with chauvinism, and where that tradition can be laid aside with glee, let us do so. But can we reach consensus concerning what is an expendable tradition and what is inviolate orthodoxy?

Undoubtedly there are yet other matters for us to discuss. But meanwhile there is next Sunday's liturgy to design, prayers of intercession to draft, hymns to select, choir music to choose. Choir music may be the most troublesome of all history to sort through, what with the library of sacred music being a magnificent repository of melody and harmony to abysmally sexist words. Much good can be accomplished by careful preaching and careful speaking. We can at least be responsible for how we presently shape our sentences, and we can wherever we are placed show concern and good will for the sisters on both sides of the argument. It is not easy to alter one's speech, but keeping one's brain ahead of one's mouth is hardly the most terrifying lion that Christians have had to face.

Meanwhile as we are doing our homework, the tradition itself gives us excellent bedtime reading. There are the psalms with their profuse imagery for God. There are the mystics like Catherine of Siena: in the close of her Dialogue she praises the Trinity not as is customary, Father, Son, and Spirit, but as fire, light, sea, abyss. There is crazy Dionysius the Areopagite, for whom God is not: not light, not fortress. There are the Christian poets: Dante can describe all those tortures of hell in splendid accuracy, but when he sees God, the circles of light with the center of flame, he complains at the incompetence of his skill with words. For as the book of the Revelation reminds us, the real name of God nobody knows. And yet we are called to worship this God whose name we cannot know, whose description we can only approximate. So while we are doing our homework, we live in hope for the end time, when we will praise this God face to face.

18
Liturgical Prayer and God as Mother

CAN LITURGICAL PRAYER ADDRESS GOD AS MOTHER? TO DATE THIS question has not been dealt with satisfactorily. Radical groups open the Lord's Prayer with "Our Mother in heaven," while some systematic theologians find in these words a revival of ancient heresies. This paper attempts to take seriously both viewpoints and, after defining terms as carefully as any seminal discussion will require, to offer the following orthodox and liberating solution: that in Lutheran liturgical prayer God the Father may and should be addressed as mother, providing that "mother" be recognized as an epithet for God and not a divine name.

The proposed discussion raises several background questions. What is Lutheranism, its source of authority, and its relation to the Christian tradition? What is liturgical prayer? Are there restrictions affecting liturgical prayer which do not apply to private prayer, mystical prayer, or poetic forms? Why has Christian tradition settled on the name Father as the primary address to God? By what other names besides Father is God addressed in liturgical prayer, and can these inform our discussion? Finally, the designation of God as mother must be considered from mythological, biblical, ecclesiastical, psychological, and modern feminist positions. The ecumenical import of our inquiry will become clear as we proceed.

A debate could arise over what is specifically Lutheran in prayer, for while Lutheranism is a self-consciously confessional movement, there is no one authority to whom such a question may be addressed. A recent exposition of *The Book of Concord*, a Lutheran collection of theological writings, calls Lutheranism "a theological movement within the church catholic,"[1] and it is that understanding which will govern the present discussion. Lutheranism is a group within the church universal which proposes that the law/gospel dialectic is a fundamental tool for "doing" orthodox Christian theology. *The Book of Concord*, which begins with the three ecumenical creeds—the Apostles, the Nicene and the Athanasian—seeks to remain orthodox in its trinitarian dogma and in its Christology. Moreover, the Reformers stressed the sole authority of Scripture in determining matters of doctrine[2] and while this principle is naive and incomplete, exegesis of appropriate texts is essential in determining Lutheran policy on the topic—the naming of God in prayer—as well as on any other. These three emphases—trinitarian dogma, Christological centrality, and biblical warrant—led to a conservative stance toward worship. The Apology to the Augsburg Confession reads: "Nothing should be changed in the accustomed rites without good reason, and to foster harmony those ancient customs should be kept which can be kept without sin or without great disadvantage."[3] Lutheranism conforms its worship as much as is theologically possible to that of the church catholic. That which tests the catholic tradition and which proposes change is the word; the word informs the liturgy so that the liturgy may manifest the word.

Little has been written on the question of prayer by Lutheran feminists. The Lutheran women at Harvard Divinity School wrote concerning sexism in connection with the proposed *Lutheran Book of Worship*: "We recognize that the 'Trinitarian' language of the Father, Son, and Holy Spirit is likely to remain until there has been further discussion."[4] It is unclear whether the

1. Eric W. Gritsch and Robert W. Jenson, *Lutheranism: The Theological Movement and Its Confessional Writings* (Philadelphia: Fortress 1976) vii.

2. Theodore G. Tappert, ed., "Formula of Concord," *The Book of Concord* (Philadelphia: Fortress 1959) 464.

3. Tappert, ed., "Apology," *The Book of Concord* 222.

4. Lutheran Women at Harvard Divinity School, "We are Concerned." Open letter to Ralph R. Van Loon, Division for Parish Services, Lutheran Church in America, n.d., p. 8.

proposed option would dispense with the Trinity or would instead search for other names. Either solution, however, would represent a fundamental departure from the Lutheranism outlined in *The Book of Concord*. Another kind of departure from historic Lutheranism is seen in a feminist proposal for a rewritten Apostles' Creed: "I believe in Jesus . . . who listened to women and liked them . . ."[5] However, without an identifiable theological position such as orthodox Lutheranism provides, there is no criterion by which to evaluate the issue. If everything is allowed, there is no objection to praying to God as mother. We seek to know whether today's confessional Lutheranism can call God mother.

There may also be a debate over what consitutes liturgical prayer. Recently traditional, formal prayers of the presiding minister have sometimes been replaced with conversational or poetic forms. Liturgical prayer, however, is the corporate prayer of the church, the collective prayer of the community gathered for word and sacrament. For this study we choose Joseph Jungmann's definition, that is, the "official prayer of the leader of the liturgical assembly."[6] Such prayer is "directed to God the Father almighty and usually, in earlier times probably without exception, in such a manner that Christ is expressly named in it as Mediator of the prayer."[7] These prayers comprise the collects (including the secret, the postcommunion and psalm prayers), the canon, the preface and the Our Father.

This most restricted definition is chosen to distinguish liturgical prayer from the liturgy's poetic formulations and exaggerated language of metaphor. The *Gloria in excelsis* calls Christ King of Glory, the *Agnus Dei* calls him Lamb of God. Communion hymns ambiguously praise the Bread of Life. The passion hymns of Fortunatus address the cross itself, and Advent's "O" antiphons call Christ Key of David and Root of Jesse. Within this tradition of metaphor in both ordinary and proper hymnody, reference to God as mother would be acceptable. There is no

5. Rachel Conrad Wahlberg, "The Woman's Creed," *Women and Worship: Rooted in the New Creation, Final Report*, ed. Constance F. Parvey (New York: Lutheran World Ministries 1977) 67–68.

6. Joseph Jungmann, *The Place of Christ in Liturgical Prayer*, 2nd rev. ed., trans. A. Peeler (Staten Island, N.Y.: Alba 1965) xiii.

7. Ibid. 114.

objection to the hymn lines "As with a mother's tender hand/
He leads His own, His chosen band" (in "All Praise to God Who
Reigns Above"). But in the presiding minister's official prayer,
imaginative metaphors are abandoned. Although we sing to the
"Dew of Heaven," we do not pray to God as Dew. Thus because
God as mother might appear in poetic hymnody does not nec-
essarily allow such usage in liturgical prayer.

Since the era of primitive Christianity, the psalms have been
the preeminent prayerbook of the church, and the psalter pattern
for naming God will prove instructive in this study. However,
the psalms are technically poems or hymns and enjoy metaphoric
liberties which the church's official prayer has never shared. For
this reason the psalms will not be considered as Christian liturgical prayer.

The liturgical prayer of the church—the prayer of Christ which
the church as his body can through baptism appropriate as its
own—differs from private, mystical, or poetic prayer. Daniel
Stevick remarks that Malcolm Boyd's and Michel Quoist's "personal prayers can show great originality, for there is no community to take into consideration."[8] An example of such private
prayer is Lady Juliana's *Revelations of Divine Love*. Juliana's profoundly moving reveries describe the second person of the Trinity as "our Mother, Brother, and Savior."[9] Juliana's identification
of Christ with the church allows her free use of mother-language
for the Son—"our Mother, Holy Church, that is, Christ Jesus."[10]
She applies the qualities of motherhood to Christ: "our
precious Mother, Jesus, He may feed us with Himself";[11]
for "our high Father . . . willeth that the Second Person
should become our Mother. Our Father willeth, our Mother
worketh . . .";[12] "So willeth He that we must do as a meek child,
saying thus: 'My kind Mother, my Gracious Mother, my dear-
worthy Mother, have mercy on me.' "[13] As with many others in

8. Daniel Stevick, *Language in Worship: Reflections on a Crisis* (New York:
Seabury 1970) 10.
9. Lady Juliana, *Revelations of Divine Love*, ed. George Warrack (London:
Methuen 1901) 145.
10. Ibid. 154–155.
11. Ibid. 150.
12. Ibid. 148.
13. Ibid. 154.

the mystical tradition, Juliana's usage was neither condemned nor adopted by the church. Her reveries, complementary to but separate from the liturgy, were seen to be too private and mystical for the "shared syntax"[14] of public worship. Further, Juliana's reveries do not provide the warrant for addressing God the Father as mother. Juliana embellishes an already existing metaphoric tradition which ascribes to the second person feminine imagery, such as Lady Wisdom and Mother Church. Liturgical prayer addressed to the first person is another matter.

There is also a sharp distinction between liturgical prayer and poetic forms. We remember John Donne's imagery of rape:

> Take me to You, imprison me, for I,
> Except You enthrall me, never shall be free,
> Nor ever chaste, except You ravish me.[15]

There are the stark lines of T.S. Eliot:

> Because these wings are no longer wings to fly
> But merely vans to beat the air
> The air which is now thoroughly small and dry
> Smaller and dryer than the will
> Teach us to care and not to care
> Teach us to sit still.[16]

Today Catherine de Vinck writes poetic prayers sharp with pained images:

> Lord, I have labored all night
> and caught nothing but ghosts on my hook.
> Give me the power to hold each thing
> named, naked, and true.[17]

14. Gracia Grindal, "Stopping by the Pit Stop," *Christian Century* 94 (1977) 454.

15. John Donne, "Holy Sonnet XIV," *John Donne's Poetry*, ed. A.L. Clements (New York: W.W. Norton 1966) 86.

16. T.S. Eliot, "Ash Wednesday," *The Complete Poems and Plays 1909–1950* (New York: Harcourt, Brace and World 1958) 61.

17. Catherine de Vinck, "Feed Me," *A Book of Uncommon Prayer* (Allendale, N.J.: Alleluia 1976) 30.

Poetic forms of prayer are personal in tone and intense in private imagery, making them inappropriate for public worship. Corporate worship must provide a common denominator: prayer which embraces all the praying people into Christ's prayer rather than luring some into a poetic vision.

Now let us examine liturgical prayer to see how it addresses God. Our data will be the pre-Vatican II Roman Sacramentary, the collection of anaphoras in *Prex Eucharistica*, and the 1978 *Lutheran Book of Worship*. This selection will demonstrate both the historic and the contemporary presiding minister's official prayer.

In the Roman Sacramentary, by far the great majority of the priest's public prayers are addressed to God simply as *Deus* or *Domine*.[18] Occasional prayers are addressed to *Pater*; yet not a single Sunday or major festival collect contains the name *Pater*. Less frequently they address *Jesu Christe*. The most common accompanying adjectives are those used in this preface formula: *Domine, sancte Pater, omnipotens aeterne Deus*. What might strike one as a lack of creativity in naming God is actually what Jungmann notes: Liturgical prayer was always strictly circumscribed by the doctrine that Christian prayer is addressed to the Father through the Son in the Spirit; and while popular piety broke this rule on occasion, for example in the *Agnus Dei* or in the *Veni Creator Spiritus*, liturgical prayer strenuously resisted such innovations.

We note that *Deus, Domine*, and *Pater* are the primary biblical names for God. "God" with its common adjective "almighty" represents the usual translation (KJV, RSV, NEB, NAB, TEV) for *El Shaddai*, God of the mountains, from Genesis 17:1 where God introduces the divine name to Abraham. The name Lord represents the traditional substitute for YHWH, the name God uses when confronting Moses in Exodus 3:14. "Father" is Scripture's own conservative translation of *Abba*, the name Jesus taught his disciples to use in prayer (Mk 14:36), which the New Testament uses increasingly in naming God. These three names, God, Lord, and Father, are the only names revealed in the Bible for the first person of the Trinity. When epithets are given (e.g., Is 6:3,

18. *The Missal in Latin and English* (Westminister, Md.: Christian Classics Catholic Booksellers 1962).

"Holy, holy, holy is the Lord of hosts," or Rv 1:8," 'I am the Alpha and the Omega,' says the Lord God, who is and who was and who is to come, the Almighty"), they are metaphors to express one aspect of the divinity named in the great revelations to Abraham, Moses and Jesus. While Jesus Christ (e.g., Jn 8:58) and the Holy Spirit (e.g., Mt 38:19) share the divine name, it is liturgical practice to address specifically the Father in prayer.

Many biblical epithets for God appear in the Roman Sacramentary, usually in apposition to a divine name, although occasionally an appropriate epithet is used alone. Some penitential prayers refer to God as Savior. A late collect praying for the pope addresses God as shepherd and ruler. Collects for saints' days elaborate this tendency: God is called "lover of virginity," "giver of strength," "author of peace." As the priest's prayers become more peripheral to corporate worship, greater liberties are allowed. The priest's vesting prayers are filled with rich metaphors: Aquinas's prayer calls Christ the pelican, and Bonaventure offers a mystical reverie: "Be thou alone always my hope and my whole confidence, my riches, my delight, my pleasure and my joy . . . my food and refreshment, my refuge and my help . . . my possession and my treasure . . ." In the hymns of the ordinary such as the *Gloria in excelsis* and in proper hymns such as the *Pange lingua, Victimae paschali,* or *Veni Creator Spiritus,* we see a wealth of metaphor characteristic of poetic forms. The movement has been biblical: while the vast majority of liturgical prayers address God by the biblically revealed names, and some prayers and the ordinary hymns use biblical epithets like King and Lamb, proper hymns become more metaphorical, and private prayers can be excessively poetic.

The eucharistic prayers are more conservative in naming God than are the shorter prayers.[19] The common preface formula is *Domine, sancte Pater, omnipotens aeterne Deus,* and in classical anaphoras these names, either alone or together, are used almost exclusively in addressing God. Although abundant metaphors are allotted to the Virgin Mary, especially in eastern anaphoras, epithets and metaphors for God are avoided in this most formal and theological part of the liturgy.

19. Anton Hänggi and Irmgard Pahl, eds., *Prex Eucharistica* (Fribourg: Editions Universitaires Fribourg 1968).

The *Lutheran Book of Worship* shows similar patterns.[20] By far the greatest number of collects are addressed either to God or to Almighty God. The name Lord occurs second in frequency. Father is used much less often, primarily in two circumstances: where the relationship to the Father to the Son is central, and where family relationships are stressed (prayers for marriage, for children). Appropriate epithets appear: "Lord our governor," in praying for those in authority, "God our creator," in praying for rural areas. Very few collects use solely an epithet. The name of God used most commonly in the liturgical texts is Lord. After the *Sanctus* the minister says "Holy God, mighty Lord, gracious Father." In the proper prefaces and ordinary hymns biblical metaphors appear: Redeemer, Word, Lamb, Most High, King.

The hymnal committee's editorial policy is evident in the psalm prayers. While not followed without exception, the intent is to distinguish names for deity from metaphor. The committee defined a name as follows: "The noun standing by itself, out of context, should be recognized as a name for deity."[21] On the other hand, nouns expressing a divine quality (fortress, bread), action (redeemer, judge), abstract idea (hope, strength), substance (one in three, life), or state (brother, king) are not capitalized, being seen as epithets found usually in apposition to a divine name: for example, "O God our light," "Lord, our refuge and strength." Very occasionally the metaphor occurs alone and, as the only noun of address, is capitalized. However, this happens so rarely that such usage is like a slip-up, surely an exception to deliberate editorial policy.

There is then, since the early church, the general rule that liturgical prayer is offered to God, especially to the first person of the Trinity, also called Lord or Father, through Jesus Christ. The subject of a prayer often suggests appropriate epithets or adjectives drawn from the numerous biblical and nonbiblical possibilities. Since it is particularly the name Father which is under scrutiny and suggests to some a warrant for using the other parental name Mother, we will now ask why Father became important in the tradition, although the data has shown that

20. *Lutheran Book of Worship* (Minneapolis: Augsburg Publishing House; Philadelphia: Board of Publication, LCA 1978).

21. Report of Language Review Committee, subcommittee of the Inter-Lutheran Commission on Worship (1975) 5–20.

Father is infrequently used in liturgical prayer. Perhaps the Lord's Prayer and the trinitarian invocation at the sign of the cross have inaccurately suggested a dominance of this name in worship. It has often been acknowledged, although it is difficult to document, that free church worship, in the absence of classical formulas, uses Father much more often in corporate prayer than do the liturgical churches. It is interesting that William Storey, in spite of his strong commitment to the elimination of sexist liturgy, urges that Father be used far more often than it has been historically, as it was Jesus' name for God.[22]

The Old Testament rarely uses father language for God but the context of the usage is most informative. It is often noted that the Canaanite sky god El was an autocratic father figure, and it is frequently assumed that this patriarchal god has considerable influence on the Hebrew picture of God.[23] However, in nearly every instance in the Old Testament, Father is a title of God available only to especially chosen and loved ones. The filial relationship is by adoption. Of Solomon, the temple builder, God promises to David: "I will be his father, and he shall be my son" (2 Sm 7:14; 1 Chr 17:13; 22:10; 28:6). Here, as in Psalm 89:26, the Davidic dynasty is called into unique relationship with YHWH: because the king is chosen to be the son of God, God is Father. Less explicit language is used of the convenant people: "Israel is my firstborn son," reads Exodus 4:22. Isaiah 63:16 and 64:8 parallel Father with Redeemer and Potter, as a repentant Israel turns back to God in prayer, acknowledging God as Father. In Jeremiah 3:19 the Lord grieves because the people scorn the covenant and refuse to call God Father, and the promise that the remnant will return repeats the formula (31:9): "for I am a father to Israel, Ephraim is my firstborn." A variation of this tradition is seen in Psalm 68:5, where God is merciful to the oppressed: God is "father of the fatherless and protector of widows." Here father probably conveys the gratuitous mercy of God rather than a formal covenant relationship.

22. William Storey, comments made in discussion session at the Valparaiso University Liturgical Institute, Valparaiso, Indiana, 25 February 1976.

23. Frank Moore Cross, *Canaanite Myth and Hebrew Epic* (Cambridge: Harvard 1973) 15–75; John Gray, *The Legacy of Canaan: The Ras Shamra Texts and Their Relevance to the Old Testament*, 2nd rev. ed. (Leiden: E.J. Brill 1965) 155–175.

The suggestion is indeed rare that God is the father of all humanity by being creator of the universe. Deuteronomy 32:6 and Malachi 2:10 seem to connect fatherhood with creation; yet in both passages the main issue is the creation of Israel as a covenant nation. Only in Malachi 1:6—"If then I am a father, where is my honor?"—is there an explicit connection between fatherhood and authority. The context of most Old Testament occurrences of Father suggests, to the contrary, that God's fatherhood is a gracious gift since it makes the covenant people, especially the king, God's children. Whatever Israel received from El, the autocratic patriarch has been radically reinterpreted as YHWH the loving Father.

Again in the apocrypha, Father is usually the distinctive name used by the covenant people. In Sirach 23 the righteous one prays to the "Lord, Father, and Ruler of my life," and to "Lord, Father, and God of my life" for strength to avoid sin. In Wisdom 2:16 the righteous one is ridiculed for calling God father; in Wisdom 11:10, while God is a severe king to the sinner, God is a father to the righteous. In Wisdom 14:3 the Father's providence consists in the power to save. This prominent Hebrew theme of God as the loving father of the adopted people extends into the intertestamental times and survives in the New Testament, where the old covenant typology of the anointed king as the adopted son of God is epitomized in Jesus' title Messiah.

Next to be noted are Jesus' prayers to God as "my Father." Joachim Jeremias contends that Jesus' use of the Aramaic *Abba* in prayer (Mk 14:36) was absolutely unique in Palestinian Judaism and as such was a distinctive claim on his part to be the one chosen by God.[24] The uniqueness of Jesus' use of *Abba* is further suggested when Paul quotes this Aramaic word in passages of his Greek letters (Rom 8:15; Gal 4:6) that treat of our union with Jesus in the Spirit as adopted children of God. In the words introducing the Lord's Prayer, *audemus dicere*, "we are bold to say," classical liturgy demonstrates a similar awareness of the privileged state of the baptized in addressing God as Father. Jeremias makes the point that *Abba* is a child's word,[25]

24. Joachim Jeremias, *The Prayers of Jesus* (Naperville, Illinois: Allenson 1967) 29, 97, 111.
25. Ibid. 59–63.

perhaps best translated Papa. One set of reasons given to explain why Jesus called God Father—God's universal love for all creatures, God's accessibility, and the patriarchal need for respect[26]—has little to do with what Old Testament messianic typology and Aramaic scholarship demonstrate.

While not even New Testament writers retain the unique tone of Jesus' address *Abba*, the fact that Jesus prayed to God as his father was increasingly important in Christian consciousness. Paul frequently uses the expression "the God and Father of our Lord Jesus Christ" (e.g., Rom 15:6; 2 Cor 1:3). By an extension of this relationship, through the Spirit received in baptism, we too are able to say "God our Father and the Lord Jesus Christ" (e.g., Rom 1:7 1 Cor 1:3). When Paul uses the word Father, in the majority of instances the name Lord Jesus Christ is grammatically connected to it. Repeated usage of the term occurs in the gospel. In Luke Jesus calls God "Father" sixteen times, in Matthew forty-three; in John the term appears 115 times. Especially in Matthew's Gospel "your heavenly Father" describes the forgiving, caring, nurturing one who chooses to love the people (e.g., Mt 6:8; 6:16; 7:11; 18:19), and this usage best recalls Jesus' use of *Abba*.

These two dominant biblical strains, the typological—the elect of Israel, especially the king, as God's children—and the theological—Jesus' intimate address to God as "my Father"—are joined by a third, increasingly philosophical usage, the trinitarian naming of God as Father to denote the origin of the Son. Rooted in those passages which describe the coming of the Son of man from the Father (e.g., Mk 8:38; Mt 16:27; Lk 10:22), this concept becomes the theme of John's Gospel, where God's name Father signifies the divine origin of Jesus Christ, the Logos (e.g., Jn 1:8; 1:14; 16:28). Here the relationship of the Father to the Son is neither adoptive and salvific nor intimate and forgiving, but essential and identity-producing. This philosophical concept of the Father as the progenitor of the Logos becomes a seminal image in credal formulations. In affirming the preexistent Christ of John's Gospel, the church stressed Christ's identity with God

26. Sharon Neufer Emswiler and Thomas Neufer Emswiler, *Women and Worship: A Guide to Non-Sexist Hymns, Prayers and Liturgies* (New York: Harper & Row 1974) 19.

as the Father's Logos, rather than Jesus' intimacy with God in prayer.

In the Apostolic Fathers we find the same four uses of the title Father. Only several times is Father equated with creator, as in 1 Clement 35:3; "The Creator and Father of eternity, the all-holy, himself knows . . ."[27] Ignatius' stress on authority shows when he admonishes the people, in Magnesians 3:1, to respect the bishop "as fully as you respect the authority of God the Father." Occasionally the concept is Hebraic, as in 1 Clement 23:1: "The all-merciful and beneficent Father has compassion on those who fear him, and with kindness and love he grants his favors to those who approach him with a sincere heart." More often we see the philosophical language at work: Diognetus 12:9 praises "the Logos through whom the Father is glorified"; Magnesians 7:2 talks of "one Jesus Christ, who came forth from one Father." However by far the most common usage by the Apostolic Fathers is the attempt to repeat Jesus' usage. Thus Ignatius: "The Father is faithful: he will answer my prayer and yours because of Jesus Christ" (Trallians 13:3); "You are dear to God, the Father of Jesus Christ" (Trallians 1:2); ". . . sing praises to the Father in Jesus Christ" (Romans 2:2). We see this also in Polycarp's prayer: "Lord God almighty, Father of your beloved and blessed servant Jesus Christ . . . , I bless you" (Martyrdom 14:2).

Beginning with the second century, the distinctly Christian usage of Father—the Hebraic sense of adoptive father and Jesus' usage of *Abba*—occur much less often in the theologians than do the mythological and the Greek concepts. More theologians spoke of God as the Father of the universe, and of all humanity as God's children. J.N.D. Kelly suggests that this occurred largely as a result of Christianity's defense against gnosticism. For example, Irenaeus combats the idea of the demiurge by describing "God the Father, increate, unengendered, invisible."[28] Sometimes in this argument against gnosticism Father denotes the entire and single godhead.[29]

27. Cyril C. Richardson, ed., *Early Christian Fathers* (New York: Macmillan 1970).

28. J.N.D. Kelly, *Early Christian Doctrines*, 2nd ed. (New York: Harper & Row 1960) 86.

29. Ibid. 108.

As the church began to formulate creeds, the trinitarian meaning of Father gained ascendancy. The creeds, an elaboration on the baptismal formula, name God as Father, Son, and Spirit, and this relational language became the primary manner of naming God in Christian doctrine. Especially in the Nicene Creed one sees orthodoxy's concern to confess the divinity of Jesus, a concern which stressed John's language of the preexistent Logos. While this concept echoed some aspects of Greek philosophy, such terminology as progenitor, logos, and power was discarded for the biblical names of Father, Son, and Spirit in articulating the trinitarian mystery. These scriptural terms capture especially the relational aspect of the Trinity: that is, the Father is the Father of the Son, the Spirit is the Spirit of the Son.

In *The Book of Concord* Luther's Small and Large Catechisms add to these various conceptions a vivid picture of God the Father as a German autocrat. Despite Luther's affectionate tone in *du leiber Gott*, God the Father is the model for the various father figures who require obedience.[30] The reason that we pray at all is obedience to the Father's command.[31] We read, "Since in this prayer we call God our Father, it is our duty in every way to behave as good children so that he may receive from us not shame but honor and praise."[32]

It is unfortunate that the New Testament use of Father became obscured in liturgical prayer. It is not the mythological notion of the creator, nor the German authority figure, nor even the Greek philosophical concept of the progenitor that is the fundamental image for Christian prayer, although to varying degrees each has taken its place in Christian theology. Indeed it is precisely these images which have accentuated sexism in the picture of the deity. In the first, the maker and bearer of all is, inappropriately, male; in the second, a patriarchal culture is made the sanctified paradigm. As to the third, collects praying for a fruitful harvest, for a productive year, for stable homes, and for fertile marriage should not use Father to suggest that God as our Father creates and rules nature and the family.

Eliminating inappropriate father-language does not imply abandoning trinitarian language. While it is outside the scope

30. Tappert, ed., "Large Catechism," *The Book of Concord* 379–389.
31. Ibid. 422.
32. Ibid. 425.

of this study to discuss the continuing need for trinitarian language, the doctrine of the Trinity remains in the twentieth century a test of Christian orthodoxy. Thus it is both desirable and essential that liturgical worship acknowledge God with the biblical names Father, Son, and Spirit. As Fleming Rutledge has written: "We are not free to alter the name of God; Scripture holds us within bounds, as Calvin says, lest we seek an 'uncertain deity by devious paths.' That is one reason that the doctrine of the Trinity is so important; it marks out for us the nature of our God in order that he may be clearly differentiated from rival non-gods."[33] Thus in liturgical prayer the use of Father within trinitarian contexts is to be continued and further clarified.

Further, liturgical worship should consciously cultivate the uniquely Christian usages of Father—the Hebrew response to God's adoption and Jesus' expression of intimacy—for example, when evoking baptism, election, redemption through Christ, the will of God, forgiveness, or gifts from God. The biblical pictures of father depict a loving, caring, nurturing one, which are qualities some refer to as feminine. In a time when society is altering its stereotypes of the father as mainly authoritarian and the mother as solely nuturing, it is illogical and self-defeating to emphasize nurturing as a woman's quality. Moreover, it is unbiblical to discard the portrait of God as loving father.

It is instructive to see how the psalms apply metaphors to the name of God. In the Psalter there are over forty nouns used as epithets for God. Some are human roles: redeemer, judge, shepherd, deliverer, guide, maker. Some are impersonal objects: shade, shield, refuge, rock, tower, song, fortress. Others are abstract nouns: hope, glory, strength. God is said to be a hiding place, to be an avenger. King, rock, and refuge are the three most common metaphors. It is thus good biblical tradition to be free and rich with metaphors in descriptions of God, some of which are as mundane as cup and tower and light.

Daniel Stevick has shown that biblical metaphors speak about both us and God simultaneously, since they describe encounter:[34] this explains the "my" in the psalms and Jesus' distinctive "my

33. Fleming Rutledge, "Thoughts on Reading the Prophet Ezekiel after Minneapolis," St. Luke's Journal of Theology 20 (1976) 24.

34. Daniel Stevick, "The Language of Prayer," Response in Worship, Music, and the Arts 16 (1976) 5–18.

Father." The metaphors are mixed freely, since no one metaphor is adequate. Most are transformational images which contrast one's old life with the new life in god, and usually—even as we saw with Father—they are tied to saving events rather than to the natural order. Finally, Stevick shows that the analogy also transforms the image. It is not that God resembles a judge; rather, in calling God a judge the Bible alters the human view of what a judge should be. Were metaphors to work in the other direction, religious language would be idolatrous, trying to depict God in human image.

Stevick uses the term metaphor to include what this study has identified as the name Father. Metaphor can be an extremely broad term. Ernst Cassirer uses the term "metaphoric thinking" to describe all human language, as he notes that the origins of language in myth are associated with the magical power of naming.[35] Within this definition all language is metaphor—not only Jesus' term *Abba*, but also the word God itself—a verbal symbol of an idea. Lord then becomes a metaphor of a metaphor, an approved symbol for that deeper, more mystifying symbol, YHWH. However appealing this use of metaphor may be, it effectively eliminates the word from critical vocabulary, and we must invent another word to name that type of figurative speech in which a word or phrase is used to create an identity or analogy between unlike things. It is this more defined literary sense of metaphor which this study uses in distinction to the word "name."

Ian T. Ramsey shows that religious language is always two-pronged: it is objective language strangely qualified. Using the terms "model" and "qualifier," he shows that the model incorporates a human category while the qualifier transforms that category into the divine.[36] Thus Father and Son are the models; "of one substance" and "eternally begotten" are the transforming qualifiers. Familiar human language is radically altered by revelation so that it can better talk about God. Thomas Fawcett and John Macquarrie describe this condition as the use of para-

35. Ernst Cassirer, *Language and Myth*, trans. Susanne K. Langer (New York: Dover 1953) 88–96.

36. Ian T. Ramsey, *Religious Language* (New York: Macmillan 1963) 183–185.

dox to correct analogy,[37] and this paradoxical nature of religious language cautions us against facilely renaming God in culturally determined models which all too often must stand without the revealed qualifier.

Robert Jenson reminds us of Aquinas' appreciation that all human language is only analogous, and he believes that twentieth century linguistic philosophy has forced Christians to account for the meaning of this analogous language.[38] Jenson grounds his explorations into religious language in the biblical narrative about Jesus: "Theological utterance is narration of the story about Jesus, qualified by and qualifying 'God.' . . . Theological utterance is narration of the story about Jesus as the story about God."[39] The paradox of Jesus' story qualifies the human conception of God and thus is the primary informant for Christian theological language.

However, even a sensitivity to paradox and an adherence to the story of Jesus do not easily resolve the problems of naming God in prayer. Within the Christian tradition the naming and describing of God are prerogatives of the sacred. God alone discloses God's name, and when humans name or describe God, the danger of idolatry is always present. It is tempting to describe God as we wish God to be, and even if our motives are the best, human thought and human language cannot capture the essence of God. Thus the Hebrews were not to draw or sculpt God nor even, at a later date, to pronounce God's proper name. When Jesus appropriates to himself the power of the divine name (Jn 8:28; 18:6), the people react with either horror or awe. The mystic tradition honors the power of God beyond language both in its practice of saying what God is not and in its respect for silence. The church of the twentieth century stands responsibly within this tradition only when it upholds in reverence the name of God and when it takes with utter theological seriousness the naming of God in prayer.

37. Thomas Fawcett, *The Symbolic Language of Religion* (London: SCM 1970) 65–67 and John Macquarrie, *God-Talk: An Examination of the Language and Logic of Theology* (London: SCM 1967) 212–230.

38. Robert W. Jenson, *The Knowledge of Things Hoped For: The Sense of Theological Discourse* (New York: Oxford 1969) 84, 106.

39. Ibid. 139.

The title "God the Mother" has an extensive history, and we could not use the term without first becoming aware of its meaning both outside and within the church. The following sketch will be chronological from the term's mythological roots through biblical and ecclesiastical uses until this century's contributions through depth psychology and the feminist movement.

Anthropologists and historians of religion commonly postulate that in primitive agricultural societies the people's primary religious allegiance was directed to an earth mother goddess who represented and insured the earth's fertility.[40] Often she was mated with a sky god, particularly manifested in the rain which nourished the crops. But the earth mother was the more fundamental, the more essential source, especially in those cultures in which the male role in procreation was not understood.[41]

When the nomadic Hebrew tribes settled in Canaan and took up agriculture, their desert god YHWH acquired new characteristics appropriate to the new situation. Simultaneously the people adopted some of the region's mother goddess cult into their lives. Probably Yahwism and the Asherah cult flourished side by side for several centuries. Joseph Campbell suggests that much of the Old Testament was a priestly attempt to elevate Yahwism over the prevailing mother goddess cults of the people.[42] Whether the priestly historians were responsible is difficult to say, since a pattern common among primitive peoples seems to have been the move from allegiance to a female earth goddess associated with local vegetation to a male sky god associated with the sun and the stars, whose sphere of influence is all-embracing and who quickly comes to signify also truth, time, wisdom, and so forth.[43] Perhaps the Canaanites' fertility myths were so powerful as to threaten Israelite identity; perhaps the cult was rejected as immoral. For whatever reasons, Yahwism became a patriarchal religion which attempted to destroy the earth goddess cult. The Books of Moses urge a total commitment

40. Joseph Campbell, *The Masks of God: Occidental Mythology* (New York: Viking 1964); Mircea Eliade, *Patterns in Comparative Religion*, trans. Rosemary Sheed (New York: New American Library, Meridian 1963); and E.O. James, *The Cult of the Mother-Goddess* (London: Thames and Hudson 1959).

41. Eliade, *Patterns in Comparative Religion* 243–244.

42. Campbell, *The Masks of God: Occidental Mythology* 100.

43. Eliade, *Patterns in Comparative Religion* 38–39, 124–126.

to the YHWH of Israel's history, and prophets inveigh against the syncretistic cult then practiced. In this effort to expunge the cult of the goddess, it is surprising that Yahwism did not become more patriarchal than it did. We have already noted how seldom YHWH is called Father, a name which, particularly due to the possible influence of Canaan's El, might have been stressed to combat the mother goddess worship.

Perhaps the main reason that the Old Testament both rejects the mother goddess and downplays the Father God is that Israel saw its god as fundamentally transcendent. Neither male nor hermaphroditic, YHWH transcended sexuality, and it was idolatrous to create God in human image. Yet the Old Testament described God in both male and female images. Phyllis Trible has demonstrated how many passages in the Old Testament depict God as a women.[44] God is never called Mother, nor does Mother ever occur in the vocative in the Old Testament. Moreover, similes of God, for example as a dragon or a thunderbolt, remind us that the biblical writers include numerous images which never prompt a vocative. Yet Trible's evidence is most instructive.

Deuteronomy 32:18 is an instance in which God is called "the Rock that begot [or bore] you . . . the God who gave you birth." Often the explicitly feminine meaning of this second verb is poorly represented in English translations, but here the Old Testament is using the myth of the creator earth goddess, just as it uses that of the creator sky god. Several other texts compare the Lord to a mother: in Isaiah 42:14 the Lord will cry out like a woman in labor; in Isaiah 49:15 the Lord's faithfulness is compared to that of a nursing mother; in Psalm 131:2 God comforts the people like a nursing mother her child; in Psalm 22:10 God takes the mother's place in caring for the psalmist. Trible suggests that the verb "to show mercy," *rhm*, is linguistically derived from the noun "womb," *rhm*, and that these ideas are presumably connected in the racial memory, so that when in many credal formulations and prophetic addresses (e.g., Ex 34:6; Ps 111:4; Jl 2:13) God is acclaimed as merciful, the feminine metaphor of the

44. Phyllis Trible, "God, Nature of, in the Old Testament," *The Interpreter's Dictionary of the Bible*, Supplementary Volume (Nashville: Abingdon 1976) 368–369.

nurturing womb is present. This may well have been true, though there is no way to prove that such an association was made by those who called God merciful. But there are the explicit passages in which God is likened to a mother bearing and nursing her child.

If God the Mother fared poorly under the Yahwists, she fared worse under the Church Fathers. New Testament feminine imagery, for example in Revelation 12, became associated with the church and was separated from and contrasted with divine imagery: the church was feminine, God was masculine. The dominant Platonist philosophy was highly sexist in its outlook, and this mentality constituted the framework into which Christianity fitted. A classic second-century Platonist text, perhaps studied by Justin Martyr, explains: "Those who permit themselves to be overcome by unrighteousness will enter, in a second existence, into the life of a woman; if they do not amend their ways, they will end by becoming animals."[45] No matter how much the biblical witness tempered this view with stories of great women and hopes of eschatological equality, the generally misogynist tone of Hellenistic philosophy marked Christian theology. Rosemary Radford Reuther has documented this philosophical tendency in the Church Fathers who intensified the primitive link between femininity and procreation by identifying spirituality with masculinity.[46] The resultant antithesis between divinity and femininity effectively eliminated feminine imagery for God.

There were specific ways the mother goddess affected the church. E.O. James discusses the Magna Mater cult in Asia Minor, a popular religious cult which, he suggests, influenced Christianity's language concerning Holy Mother Church and Mary the Mother of God.[47] Exceedingly important in the first few centuries of Christianity was gnostic Christianity's assimilation of mother goddess imagery into the biblical divinity. Elaine Pagels documents those Christian gnostics who variously fit the feminine into the godhead; for example, in the *Secret Book of John*

45. Albinus, "Summary of the Teachings of Plato," trans. R.A. Norris Jr. (mimeo) ch. 21:2, p. 21.

46. Rosemary Radford Ruether, "Misogynism and Virginal Feminism in the Fathers," *Religion and Sexism: Images of Women in the Jewish and Christian Traditions*, ed. R. Ruether (New York: Simon and Schuster 1974) 150–179.

47. James, *The Cult of the Mother-Goddess* 192–203.

the Spirit becomes the mother, while in the *Great Announcement* the Son as Sophia is the divine mother.[48] Pagels concludes as follows:

> The evidence does indicate that two very different patterns of sexual attitudes emerged in orthodox and gnostic circles. In simplest form, gnostic theologians correlate their description of God in both masculine and feminine terms with a complementary description of human nature. . . This conception carries the principle of equality between men and women into the practical social and political structures of gnostic communities. The orthodox pattern is strikingly different: it describes God in exclusively masculine terms . . . Like the gnostic view, the orthodox also translates into sociological practice: by the late second century, orthodox Christians came to accept the domination of men over women as the proper, God-given order—not only for the human race, but also for the Christian churches.[49]

Irenaeus is among those who condemn gnosticism for other than sexist reasons. In *Against Heresies* he opposes what he recognizes as untrue invention in gnostic myth and departure from biblical sources and traditional Christian expression. His understanding of God's transcendence makes him abhor myths making God a hermaphrodite.[50] His specific comments about the mother goddess suggest not a sexist bias so much as a biblical and traditional bias,[51] for he sees the proliferation of novel gods as a refusal by gnostic Christianity to take seriously the doctrine of the incarnation. Irenaeus represents the historic tradition of theologians who discard an idea like God the Mother largely because it is an innovation.

Gregory of Nazianzus addresses the issue from a different viewpoint. An intellectual, he ridicules the idea that the gender associated with the name of God somehow implies sexuality:

> Maybe you would consider our God to be a male, according to the same arguments, because he is called God and Father, and that

48. Elaine Pagels, "What Became of God the Mother? Conflicting Images of God in Early Christianity," *Signs: Journal of Women in Culture and Society* 2 (1976) 293–303; cf, pp. 295, 297.

49. Ibid. 301–302.

50. Irenaeus, *Against Heresies*, trans. Edward Rochie Hardy, *Early Christian Fathers*, ed. Cyril C. Richardson (New York: Macmillan 1970) 364.

51. Ibid. 379.

deity is feminine, from the gender of the word, and Spirit neuter, because it has nothing to do with generation; but if you would be silly enough to say with the old myths and fables, that God begot the Son by a marriage with his own will, we should be introduced to the hermaphrodite god of Marcion and Valentinus who imagined those newfangled Aeons.[52]

This issue is echoed today when Spirit is rendered feminine due to the Hebrew word of feminine gender, *rûah*. Yet while it may be difficult for systematicians to admit, there is no doubt that the use of the names Father and Son, titles like King and Lord, and the male pronoun have framed in the mind of the average Christian the image of a male god. In hoping to avoid a hermaphroditic god, western Christianity has drawn a male god.

Yet feminine imagery for God appears in scattered places in the tradition. Most notable, along with Juliana, is Clement of Alexandria. Especially in *The Instructor* he presents a long comparison of the Word with milk; the Father thus becomes the nursing mother. He calls Christ "the nourishing substance of milk swelling out of breasts of love."[53] God is "the nourisher and the Father of all that are generated and regenerated."[54] Note two other examples: "We, believing on God, flee to the Word, the 'care-soothing breast' of the Father. And He alone, as is befitting, supplies us children with the milk of love, and those only are truly blessed who suck this breast."[55] "To us infants, who drink the milk of the Word of the heavens, Christ Himself is food. Hence seeking is called sucking; for to those babes that seek the Word, the Father's breasts of love supply milk."[56] It is unfortunate that this metaphoric language, based soundly on biblical imagery, is so rare in the tradition.

Depth psychology offers a critique of Christianity's metaphorical male god. Carl Jung bemoans the lack of the feminine

52. Gregory of Nazianzus, "The Fifth Theological Oration: On the Spirit," *Christology of the Later Fathers*, Vol. III, *Library of Christian Classics*, ed. Edward R. Hardy and Cyril C. Richardson (Philadelphia: Westminster 1954) 298.

53. Clement of Alexandria, *The Instructor, the Ante-Nicene Fathers*, Vol. II, ed. Alexander Roberts and James Donaldson (Grand Rapids, Mich.: Eerdmans 1951) 218.

54. Ibid. 219.

55. Ibid. 220.

56. Ibid. 221.

in the Christian God and suggests that the doctrine of the assumption of Mary was the initial step in introducing the feminine into the godhead.[57] However, in his search for a totality within God, his discussion of the feminine as an antithesis to the masculine becomes confused with his discussion of the devil as an antithesis to God, and we have not made progress if whatever is feminine in the deity is identified as evil. Ann Ulanov provides a more thorough discussion of the feminine in God. She writes that a balanced view of life must contain the polarity of masculine and feminine, rather than what has been common in the church, a polarization between them.[58] Christian mystics celebrated this polarity in their sexual metaphors of the soul's meeting with God, but in the mainstream of the tradition there has been a suppression of the feminine in religious symbolism which "leads to suppression of the feminine in human life, which means suppression of the main appearance of otherness in our daily lives,"[59] resulting in psychological immaturity and imbalance. In hope that western religion can get beyond the patriarchal stage, Ulanov cites Paul Tillich's image of the Ground of Being with its "mother quality of giving birth, carrying, and embracing"[60] as an appropriate Christian image.

However attractive this Jungian desire for balanced polarity to express totality adequately, the question of how the feminine can be introduced into liturgical prayer remains. Some writers urge the use of both Mother and Father in prayer, as in "Mother and Father God," but prefer nongender titles, as relational titles are "too influenced by one's own biography."[61] The editors of the collection *Sistercelebrations* "selected a trinitarian formula developed earlier for a Lutheran women's service: 'In the name of God, the mother and father of all life . . .' "[62] But the Christian God is related to the worshiper through adoption by faith, not

57. C.G. Jung, "A Psychological Approach to the Dogma of the Trinity," trans. R.F.C. Hull, *Psychology and Religion: West and East*, Vol. III, *Collected Works* (Princeton: Princeton University Press 1969) 171.

58. Ann Belford Ulanov, *The Feminine in Jungian Psychology and in Christian Theology* (Evanston: Northwestern University Press 1971) 296.

59. Ibid. 318.

60. Ibid. 109.

61. Sharon and Thomas Neufer Emswiler, *Women and Worship* 24.

62. Arlene Swindler, ed., *Sistercelebrations* (Philadelphia: Fortress 1974) 36.

through ownership by creation. As Athanasius wrote: "Christians seem to be more immediately interested and concerned in the belief and confession of God's paternity than of his creatorship . . . The Gentiles, who were altogether strangers to the Son, were the authors of the word Unmade; whereas our Lord himself commonly spoke of God in the style of Father and has taught us in like manner to use and apply the word."[63]

An article in *Dialog* suggested that the personal intimacy inherent in Jesus' use of *Abba* can no longer be represented by the English word Father, and that Parent should be used instead.[64] The author, likening the oddness of the use of Parent with the oddness of Jesus' use of *Abba*, does not realize that the scandal of Jesus' terminology lay in its excessive intimacy, while the oddness of Parent lies in its total lack of intimacy. The suggestions of Mother-Father and Parent, while ill-advised, at least attempt to deal with feminist concerns from within the tradition.

Radical feminists are less convinced that their concerns can be congruent with orthodox Christianity. Mary Daly's chapter "Beyond Christology" states, "The growing woman-consciousness is in conflict with fundamentalist and orthodox doctrines concerning Jesus," and "women can look neither to Catholicism nor Protestantism for adequate models of liberation."[65] Daly rejects Christian models and calls a feminist liturgy "a contradiction in terms . . . an attempt to put new wine, women's awareness, into the old skins of forms that kill female self-affirmation and turn female consciousness against itself."[66] A less extreme position, that of Elisabeth S. Fiorenza, states that "the stuff of feminist liturgies is women's experience and women's life"[67] and that we must "be careful not to *equate* God with female images, in order that Christian women remain free to transcend the 'fem-

63. Athanasius, "First Oration Against the Arians," *Four Orations Against the Arians*, trans. Samuel Parker (London: Oxford 1713) 69–71.

64. H. Paul Santmire, "Retranslating 'Our Father': The Urgency and the Possibility," *Dialog* 16 (1977) 102.

65. Mary Daly, *Beyond God the Father: Toward a Philosophy of Women's Liberation* (Boston: Beacon 1973) 72 and 85.

66. Ibid. 145.

67. Elisabeth S. Fiorenza, "Feminist Theology as a Critical Theology of Liberation," *Theological Studies* 36 (1975) 616.

inine' images and roles of our culture."[68] Another woman wrote that feminist theology is an alternative to traditional, that is, sexist, theology;[69] in feminist theology woman centers in herself rather than in man, whether that be Christ or her husband.

Keeping in mind both the orthodox necessity of father language and the past and present meanings of mother imagery, we must now explore the possibility of a new theological statement, the affirmation that God the Father can be mother. Langdon Gilkey offers three criteria for any theological statement: (1) the statement must be a consistent expression of the symbolic forms of the historic Christian community; (2) it must be related and relevant to the actual questions of our existence; and (3) it must be validated "by its width of relevance and its adequacy of explanatory power."[70] These three tests—historicity, relevance, and universality—shall frame our question: can liturgical prayer address God as Mother?

The first question asks whether God the Mother is consistent with the symbolic forms of the historic Christian community. In light of the biblical and ecclesiastical evidence, we would judge that Mother cannot be used as a name for God. Revealed tradition has not legitimized this name as a name for the Christian God. It is not used once in the Bible. The recasting of the Lord's Prayer to read "Our Mother in heaven" dismisses the Bible's and the church's traditions and would be unacceptable in Lutheran liturgical prayer.

However, God *as mother* is a wholly different matter. The Bible uses this metaphor; the psalms legitimize it and address God with various anthropomorphic and objectifying terms. Clement of Alexandria offers striking examples. Furthermore, it is true to the biblical spirit that the church guard against any idolatrous imaging of God. At this time in history, the refusal to adopt the metaphor mother appears in many cases to be a subtle idolatry which construes God as male. The principle of paradox in biblical descriptions of God, in which God is both father and heavenly,

68. Ibid. 624.

69. Eleanor Haney, "God and Wo/man: A Feminist Perspective," *Dialog* 16 (1977) 182.

70. Langdon Gilkey, *Naming the Whirlwind: The Renewal of God-Lanuage* (Indianapolis: Bobbs-Merrill 1969) 460–463.

both Father and Son, urges the church to balance its own always inadequate language for God by further employing paradox. The mystics acknowledge this principle when they claim that God is silence and darkness. The same paradox is operative when Juliana calls God the Son her mother. The paradoxical manner in which God is described would alone encourage the metaphor mother for God.

The second test is one of relevance. It is a growing consensus that Christianity has too completely and too long concurred in the sexism of the western world, and in no small part this has occurred because God has been construed as male. Incorporating the metaphor of God as mother would help to set the prayer language of the church in a more respectable position. The current effort of feminists to alert the church to its sexism too often results only in polarization. Mary Daly's work, *The Church and the Second Sex* (1968), was one such moderate attempt. Her radical *Beyond God the Father* (1973) demonstrates her rage at the insensitivity with which she was met. It is likely that much remaining resistance to women's ordination stems from the unconscious identification of God with men and thus of men with God. Today's request by women cannot be ignored by the church, and incorporation of feminine images for God could play at least a small part in rectifying centuries of distortion and error.

The third question is one of universality: "its width of relevance and its adequacy of explanatory power."[71] In other words, how well does this language work for how many people? God as mother will have to be introduced carefully into liturgical worship so that it involves a wide spectrum of people. When it is brazenly propagated, it strikes too many worshipers as a purely political move. Don Saliers wrote that we cannot try "to make worship palatable or exciting simply by employing the latest pop-culture jargon or trappings."[72] Rather, in the historic collect tradition, the prayer must use the metaphor to illuminate a biblical truth about God which informs the prayer's specific petition. When used responsibly the metaphor mother can become relevant to many.

71. Gilkey, *Naming the Whirlwind* 463.
72. Don E. Saliers, "On the 'Crisis' of Liturgical Language," *Worship* 44 (1970) 410.

The attendant question of universality involves the adequacy of the symbol. No single image is sufficient to describe deity. The psalms show that the people's praise is always searching creatively for metaphors which express new facets of the revelation. We do not suggest that mother is the complete or even the primary metaphor for the Christian God. Further, the symbol would be inadequate from the start if human discriptions of mother inform the metaphor. In addressing God as mother, we are not praying to a primitive earth goddess, to the mate of a sky god, to Sophia, to Jung's eternal feminine principle, or to what the contemporary world might construe as an ideal mother. Nor are we copying Juliana in naming Christ our mother. The symbol will be as adequate a description of deity as is possible only if it is drawn from the biblical witness.

In conclusion we offer the following collects as examples of what ought to be incorporated regularly into Lutheran liturgical prayer.

On the reception of the word: "O God, you are a nursing mother to all your faithful people. Nourish us with the milk of your word that we may live and grow in you, through your Son Jesus Christ our Lord."

On the benefits of the eucharist: "O God our Father, our mother and our nurse, in baptism you have given us life through the death of your Son. Feed us now with your bread and wine that we may receive and be his body in the world, through whom we pray."

On God's gift of mercy: "O God, you are a merciful mother to us; with suffering you brought your people to birth, and with compassion you raise us up in your way. Nurture us with your Spirit's life that we may be your children, to live out the praise for which we were born, through your Son Jesus Christ our Lord."

These prayers are an attempt to follow scriptural metaphors rather than cultural suggestions in determining the use of feminine images. Specifically, for example, God as mother relates to our reception of the word, not to our observance of Mother's Day or to our acceptance of women's liberation. The solution here suggested to this one dilemma of sexism in liturgy will perhaps please systematicians more than feminists. However, the solution represents an honest attempt to deal with issues that are far more complex than the popular rhetoric of either side admits. The author stands ready, as ought the whole church, to listen to any response in a continual search for the always faithful and liberating will of God in this age.[73]

73. Author's note. This article was written in 1978. I stand behind the data, but I no longer argue its categories or precise conclusion.

19

De Divinis Nominibus:
The Gender of God

HOW DOES HUMAN LANGUAGE NAME GOD? WHICH REVEALED WORDS
has the tradition canonized, and how do the faithful verbally
express and interpret their relationship with God? "You shall
not make for yourself a graven image," it was said. Yet more
solid than stone, more resistant to iconoclasm than bronze, are
the images cast in theological language and so engraved on our
minds and throughout our prayers. We must always be inquiring
whether the tendency of theological language toward immuta-
bility is wholly a healthy one. It is to that theological language
which names God as "he" that this inquiry is addressed.

   With the phrase *de divinis nominibus*, on the divine names, we
recall both Dionysius and Thomas Aquinas.[1] It is with both that
we must converse, the elaborate metaphors of Christian imagery
and the reasoned discourses of systematic theologians. We know
that Christian poets and mystics have a rare ability to talk to and
of God in unique ways. But by definition their vision is a private
one, and while we admire Dionysius' *via negativa* or Julian of
Norwich's praise of Jesus as Mother, we do not employ their
writings in public prayer. Offshoots of Christianity more intrigued by metaphor than by dogma enjoy a release from canonized language, but the gnostics were anathematized, the
Shakers have died out, and Jung was hardly a worshiping church
member. Heinrich Ott's recent theological study of God as per-

1. Thomas Aquinas, *Summa Theologiae* 1a. 13, 1.

son notes correctly that problems in naming God arise in conversation *about* God. Hence he urges conversation *to* God.[2] Yet he writes about the safety of direct address in language which is unquotably sexist. We are responsible at least for the language we engrave on the minds and prayers of others. While like the Cistercians we realize the inadequacy of language, we must also like the Cistercians choose some language with which to pray faithfully.

Conversations about the naming of God as Father are becoming increasingly common,[3] and recently publications have pointed to the difficulty in calling God "he."[4] But serious investigation into the gender of God has not proceeded very far. About God's gender it is far easier to hold an impassioned opinion than to articulate a reasoned argument or a reasonable solution. This study will address the "God-he" problem with the following questions: How does language talk of God? How has the Judeo-Christian tradition named God's gender, and why? How does gender function in modern American English? What are the alternatives to calling God he? If we agree that refusing to examine our engraved speech leads to an idolatry more sophisticated but no less culpable than that with the golden calf, we have at least begun at the same place.

"All I have written seems to me like so much straw compared with what I have seen and what has been revealed to me." With these words Thomas Aquinas admitted the inadequacy of words to describe God, and he ceased work on the *Summa Theologiae.* While some may suggest that we need no words to address God in the interior of our heart, human beings do require words at least to talk together to and of God. In searching for the best words to use, we turn first to Thomas' discussion of theological

2. Heinrich Ott, *God,* tr. Iain and Ute Nicol (Atlanta: John Knox 1974).

3. For example: *God as Father?* ed. Johannes-Baptist Metz and Edward Schillebeeckx, *Concilium* 143 (New York: Seabury 1981), and Krister Stendahl, "Enrichment or Threat? When the Eves Come Marching In," *Sexist Religion and Women in the Church: No More Silence!* ed. Alice Hageman (New York: Association 1974) 117–123.

4. Letty Russell, "Changing Language and the Church," *The Liberating Word* (Philadelphia: Westminster 1976) 92–93; Marianne Sawicki, *Faith and Sexism: Guidelines for Religious Educators* (New York: Seabury 1979) 19–23.

language. For despite his final disclaimer of language, and despite his sexism much derided by shocked moderns, he investigates the naming of God with a clarity which has undergirded all subsequent inquiry. For critical historical study has shown that a thinker can be entirely brilliant on one subject—say, linguistic philosophy—while being completely wrongheaded on another—say, women.

How does language talk of God? In the linguistic philosophy of the ancient Near East, a thing had no reality prior to its naming. This theory has been adapted in modern philosophy as the theory of the interrelationship between language and reality. That is, we know as we name. But God, Genesis claims, is prior to language. The divine is beyond the human, outside our categories. In some religions the sacred is held so far beyond the secular that a wholly separate language is employed for worship and theology. But the self-revelation of our God in history and the incarnation of Christ Jesus encourages Christians to talk of God in their finest vernacular speech.

One recent study of God's gender suggests that modern Christianity can talk directly of God and so need not use anthropomorphisms in worship and theology.[5] Besides sounding naively optimistic about human maturity, this suggestion has not deeply understood language. Human language cannot express the essence of God, nor its power effect communication with God, any more than the human mind can grasp at divinity. Different languages and genres use various techniques to varying degrees in their worship and theology. Aquinas begins his discussion of theological language by describing metaphoric use of language, and we shall begin with him there.

"Holy Scripture delivers spiritual things to us beneath metaphors taken from bodily things."[6] We talk of divine truth as though human categories applied; thus we are talking of two quite different things—the human and the divine—simultaneously. Theological language is to great degree metaphoric talk: language which is open to associations, which encourages in-

5. Sheila D. Collins, *A Different Heaven and Earth* (Valley Forge, Penn.: Judson 1974) 217.
6. Aquinas, *Summa* 1a. 1, 9.

sight and facilitates disclosure by its linking of disparate things.[7] "God is said to have no name, or to be beyond naming, because his essence is beyond what we understand of him and the meaning of the names we use."[8] We speak the metaphors with utter humility, believing in the God beyond the words and concluding our metaphoric speech to be so much straw.

Metaphors can be anthropomorphic. That is, we can talk of God as though God were a woman or a man or a child or a people. We ascribe to God breasts or a strong arm or a shining countenance. We use personification when we ascribe to God personal characteristics: anger, delight, speech, age. Nonhuman metaphors are common in the Judeo-Christian tradition. Interestingly, we speak of God as an animal or a natural phenomenon more easily than as a woman: God has wings, God belches fire. The psalms were bold in objectifying divinity. "Rock" recurs often in the psalms as a metaphor for God.

Aquinas offers metaphoric language the test of contradictability. "It is part of the meaning of 'rock' that it has its being in a merely material way. Such words can be used of God only metaphorically."[9] God is a rock: but of course God is *not* a rock. Nor has God a shining countenance or milk-filled breasts. The power of metaphor can tease us into believing the reality of our human language, and the East has employed more than the West the *via negativa*, the God-is-not speech. But even if we say God is not light, the technique of objectification is present despite the disclaimer.

Literature professors teach the proper interpretation of metaphoric language. The reader must be honest to the metaphor and not press it beyond its intent. "We are the hollow men / We are the stuffed men / Leaning together / Headpiece filled with straw"[10] does not imply that we are literally scarecrows. Nor does metaphoric talk of God as mother mean that in any essential way God is half female or acts in some stereotypically

7. Mark Searle, "Liturgy as Metaphor," *Worship* 55 (1981) 98–120; Gail Ramshaw Schmidt, "Liturgy as Poetry: Implications of a Definition," *Living Worship* 15 (October 1979) no. 8.

8. Aquinas, *Summa* 1a. 13, 1.

9. Aquinas, *Summa* 1a. 13, 4.

10. T.S. Eliot, "The Hollow Men," *The Complete Poems and Plays 1909–1950* (New York: Harcourt, Brace and World 1958) 60.

feminine manner. We must be careful of anecdotes about God's sitting up in the sky on his throne or pictures of God as two men and an amorphous third. Metaphoric language must always be contradicted. God is like a father, but a father who wills his son to die. God is like a castle: but as my two-year-old retorted, "God is not a castle. God is God."

In some contexts, naming God "he" is metaphoric. Sustained metaphors which liken God to a king might use "he" in the same metaphoric fashion (although "sovereign" sounds more noble and as a nonsex-specific noun would not require a "he"). Our recognizing the metaphoric nature of God-he language would be facilitated if we used God-she in similar constructions. It is God as she who calls us into the ways of wisdom. But the possibilities of this metaphoric language are limited. Too easily most human occupations—shepherd, judge, teacher—are assigned male pronouns, and objectifications are often assigned male pronouns, as in "Refuge, he." If only images of motherhood are granted female pronouns, we remain impoverished.[11] But even when the metaphoric use of pronouns is employed most creatively, there is still the contradictability: God is not he, God is not she.

Yet we must be bolder in our use of metaphors for God. In the disclosure of surprising metaphors we meet God anew. The startling language invites us to conversion. Reviving biblical metaphors ought not be as controversial or risky as it apparently is. To ascribe to God a full range of human activity and emotions; to balance in God the strength of God who reigns with the weakness of God who suffers; to objectify God; and finally to negate these images, pleading God-is-not: opening up God language will combat the incipient idolatry in one's traditional speech.

A second way that language talks of God is analogical. By analogy Aquinas means those verbal expressions by which we are trying to say what we mean. Of these statements one does not postulate the opposite. "Words like 'good' and 'wise' when used of God do signify something God really is, but they signify it imperfectly because creatures represent God imperfectly."[12]

11. Rita M. Gross, "Steps Toward Feminine Imagery of Deity in Jewish Theology," *Judaism* 30 (1981) 190–192.
12. Aquinas, *Summa* 1a. 13, 2.

Our saying "God is good" is not countered by our saying "God is not good." Although our category "good" is inadequate to attach to God, we use such analogical language because through it we try to speak what we mean. Aquinas insists that in analogy the Christian revelation establishes the definition, and not the other way around. That is, we look to the Scriptures for a description of God as good, from which we arrive at our definition of good. This adaptation of Platonic idealism acts to correct our natural error of imagining a God in our own image and within our own language.

We are to be humble about language even in its most careful, creedal usage. God is called Father not, as a prominent fundamentalist preacher recently announced, because otherwise the American family structure will further erode. Rather, God is named Father because in the revealed tradition Jesus called God Abba, and to that extraordinary religious event we struggle to attach human words. In the inaccurate translation of Abba into Father we see that human words are a far cry from the divine reality revealed in the seminal stories of the faith.

Trinitarian language is analogous language. The naming of the three persons of the Trinity, the calling of relationships within God, uses language which tries to say God's self-naming. All relational language concerning God is analogous. When we say that God relates not only within God's self but also with humankind, we use analogous language. Some usages of God-he language are similarly analogous. The revelation says that the Judeo-Christian God is a relational being, a God known as who, not which. The tradition has tried to say this by rejecting the pronoun "it" and using instead "he," always in this analogous usage recognized as a nonsex-specific but personal pronoun. While we can appreciate the historic intent of this language, it remains to be seen whether it is any longer possible.

Only when analogy, as Wolfhart Pannenberg says, opens up to mystery, only when our language of God leads to awed doxology, are we recognizing the limits of human language in its speech of God.[13] When in a homily an anecdote about a father-child relationship or about the birth process affirms a basic sim-

13. Wolfhart Pannenberg, "Analogy and Doxology," *Basic Questions in Theology*, tr. George H. Kehm (Philadelphia: Fortress 1972) 1, 215.

ilarity with God, the simile has shrunk our God. Always in analogy what is unlike is more than what is like. Theological sensitivity in explicating analogical language frees us from distortions and helps point to the glory of God. If we would grant often in our speech that "he" is wholly inadequate as a personal pronoun in referring to God, much of our difficulty would be lessened. Instead, we hear vociferous defense of this masculine designation, as if it were in some way true.

Edward Schillebeeckx talks of the kerygma breaking the human models.[14] He sees that human language has developed God talk, but that Christianity breaks apart that language even while being required to use it. With Jesus, he writes, we use the models of messiah or of wisdom; yet the models are admittedly inadequate, and even in some cases inappropriate, to the reality made known in Christ. So with all God talk: the models provided by human speech are recast by the proclamation of our God. It is not only, as Ian Ramsey notes, that paradox exists within the parts of the divine title, that "God" and "Father" are opposite to one another and stand in creative tension.[15] It is even, Schillebeeckx would say, that the meanings of the individual words are shattered, that "God" and "Father" are broken by the reality of the cross. It is time that we examine the model of God-he for its undoing by the cross.

Several recent studies provide thorough discussions of how God's gender was expressed throughout the Judeo-Christian tradition. Leonard Swidler offers a concise treatment of the relationship between the worship of Yahweh and of Asherah and then lists biblical, extrabiblical, rabbinic, and historic Christian references to the "feminine" aspect of God.[16] Other scholars have tried to account for the pattern of masculine language for God.[17]

14. Edward Schillebeeckx, *Interim Report on the Books Jesus and Christ* (New York: Crossroad 1981) 24, passim.

15. Ian Ramsey, *Religious Language* (New York: Macmillan 1963) 203–205.

16. Leonard Swidler, *Biblical Affirmations of Woman* (Philadelphia: Westminster 1979) 21–73.

17. For example: Paul D. Hanson, "Masculine Metaphors for God and Sex-Discrimination in the Old Testament," *The Ecumenical Review* 27 (1975) 317–321, and Elaine H. Pagels, "What Became of God the Mother? Conflicting Images of God in Early Christianity," *Womanspirit Rising: A Feminist Reader in Religion,* ed. Carol P. Christ and Judith Plaskow (New York: Harper and Row 1979) 107–119.

While this essay cannot be the place for a detailed historical study, we can review the most important aspects of the history of the naming of God's gender.

All the languages formative in the Judeo-Christian tradition had grammatical gender. That is, all nouns and pronouns were assigned, either naturally, logically, or arbitrarily, to grammatical categories called gender. Sometimes a noun's grammatical gender was elaborated upon for poetic purposes, and sometimes we can guess why a certain inanimate object was assigned its specific gender. But in languages with grammatical gender there is no actual significance in gender designation. That a table is feminine does not mean that the table has female sexuality or that it is necessarily related to a characteristically feminine realm. Hebrew, Aramaic, Greek, and Latin all have grammatical gender. In polytheistic cultures, the assigning of masculine gender to the word god is evident from the word goddess, which, as in poet-poetess, is a diminutive form. Perhaps the cultural pattern of male domination in religious matters was a, or the, significant cause. But it remains that the assignment of masculine grammatical gender does not prove anything about a supposed sexuality of the Judeo-Christian God. Hebrew and Christian theologians insisted that their God was not of one or both sexes but was beyond sexuality. Gregory of Nazianzus addresses specifically the question of masculine gender of God and ridicules those who would draw from the gender designation a notion of actual sexuality within God.[18] Aquinas, also, in defending the expression "He who is" as the most appropriate name for God, states that the term "does not signify any particular form, but rather existence itself."[19] Aquinas assumes here that the pronoun "he" does not suggest the form of the human male.

A second important aspect of the historic situation is that in the ancient world, the Judeo-Christian God stands counter to polytheism, in which there was a powerful supply of female gods. In both the Old and New Testaments, Yahweh God, the Father of Jesus Christ, opposes a significant cult of the female god, and the biblical proclamation includes polemic against the

18. Gregory of Nazianzus, "The Fifth Theological Oration: On the Spirit," *Christology of the Later Fathers*, The Library of Christian Classics, Vol. 3, ed. E.R. Hardy and C.C. Richardson (Philadelphia: Westminster 1954) 198.

19. Aquinas, *Summa* 1a. 13, 11.

sexual rituals offered before the female god. We are now studying the effects of this situation on the proclamation. Furthermore, the written documents and the cultural patterns within which Judaism and Christianity developed indicate a deeply engrained sexism, and we are only beginning to estimate to what degree and in what ways this cultural sexism influenced theological thought and expression.

Recent studies are showing us the openness of this sexist tradition to feminine gender for God. There are the oft-cited biblical references to God as woman. Jewish tradition, in its reluctance to speak directly of God, relied increasingly in its speech on feminine personifications of God. Law is hypostatized as Torah, God's presence as *shekinah*, wisdom as *hokmah*, and spirit as *ruah*. We do not know, however, how much the female personifications of these words affected theology and proclamation. It is not clear how this tradition can be imported into modern English, in which these words are not in any respect "feminine." The pattern remained, even in this tradition, that a masculine god possessed feminine characteristics. Finally, while it is illuminating and potentially corrective to read about deviant traditions, like the gnostics, the Jewish mystics, and the Shakers, in which radical measures were tried in the naming of God's gender, the idiosyncracies of those traditions make any appropriation of their attempts unrealistic.

Recent use of the word person in association with God has unfortunately tightened the tie between God and male sexuality. In the classic Christian formulations, the word person was a technical term which meant something like mode of being. God has three persons: that is, God has three ways of being within the one being of God. There are relationships within God. Language of Father and Son had to do with relations within the being of God, not with relationships between God and the faithful.

But in the last century theology has spoken of God as personal, and even of God as person. At the start this reflected relationships between God and humankind. But increasingly talk of God as person is influenced by modern definitions of person as a self-conscious being, and different theologians can stress quite different things when referring to God as person. Ott refers to

God's mutuality with humankind.[20] Pannenberg defines God's personhood as God's nonmanipulability (a highly rationalistic definition of person, I might add).[21] But language of God as person can lead to images of God as a superperson, and then all too easily to God as a supermale. Finally the word person is linked in modern American English to human personality, and we find ourselves open to anthropomorphism of the cheapest sort.

In recent debates concerning the ordination of women a dangerous example of this erroneous use of person surfaced. The priest's likeness to Christ spilled over into talk of the priest as a symbol of God, and thus male sexuality is linked not only to Christ, but in some essential way also to God.[22] But Richard Norris outlines the creedal understanding of unity in the godhead and demonstrates that even the sexuality of the man Jesus has no essential significance in the being of God.[23] It would seem as if agreement on this is possible: that while some languages assign the word God a gender, there is no sexuality—male, female, or both—inherent in the Judeo-Christian God; that any metaphoric statements which suggest such sexuality must be qualified; and that all analogical statements must be explicated in light of the theological assertion that God is beyond sexuality.

What of gender in modern American English? Anglo-Saxon, the linguistic family spoken in the British Isles in the year 1000, was an inflected language with grammatical gender like its Germanic antecedents. Into Anglo-Saxon came the Christian God, talked of in masculine gender, so translated from the Christian parent languages. Through the centuries English has become a less and less inflected language. We have now only vestiges of the old system of declining nouns and pronouns and conjugating verbs. One grammatical variable which has been almost completely abandoned is gender. Nouns no longer are arbitrarily assigned to categories called gender which influence pronoun

20. Ott, *God* 42.

21. Pannenberg, *Basic Questions*, 1, 232.

22. Urban T. Holmes, "The Feminine Priestly Symbol and the Meaning of God," *The Saint Luke's Journal of Theology* 17 (1974) 7.

23. Richard A. Norris Jr., "Priesthood and the 'Maleness' of Christ: Trinity and Christology in the Fathers," *Pro and Con on Ordination of Women*, Report and Papers from the Anglican-Catholic Consultation, 75–76.

selection and verb endings through rules of agreement. Modern American English functions almost totally with what grammarians call natural gender. That is, an animate female is "she," an animate male is "he," and all singular else is "it."

Language guidelines of publishing houses, especially those houses which produce children's books and texts, indicate the state of the language with regard to gender. Of course such thoroughgoing alterations of the gender system are not already commonplace in America. But we see a movement, legislated in some significant places, further to remove gender considerations in American English. The guidelines of publishers like Macmillan and McGraw-Hill make the following policies.[24] "man" and its compounds are no longer acceptable as generic terms; words like ship and country are "it," not "she"; occupations are not to be typecast by sex; occupational titles must not be sex-specific (except for sperm-donor and wet-nurse!); human emotions and manners of behavior are not to be stereotyped by sex; female gender word forms (poetess) are to be abandoned. These guidelines say of the "generic he" that it is no longer acceptable; the sentence can be reworded or cast into the plural; "he" can be replaced by "one" or "he or she" (as in "one or the other"); "he" might alternate with "she." An indication of the force of these moves is the 1977 statement by the National Council of Teachers of English, saying that except in the most strictly formal usage, "their" is preferable to "his" as a singular possessive pronoun.[25]

Perhaps the insularity of the church has allowed this development to catch us unprepared. Are the clergy who preach about "man's salvation" aware that the children no longer define "man" to mean "human being"? Both simple and radical alterations of our speech are being called for. For example, since God is not a male being, there is no need for the word goddess. Furthermore, "masculine" and "feminine" are difficult terms,

24. "Guidelines for Equal Treatment of the Sexes in McGraw-Hill Book Company Publications," McGraw-Hill 1974; "Guidelines for Creating Positive Sexual and Racial Images in Educational Materials," Macmillan 1975; "Eliminating Stereotypes," Houghton Mifflin 1981; and "Guidelines for Improving the Images of Women in Textbooks," Scott, Foresman and Company 1974.

25. Alleen Pace Nilsen, et al, *Sexism and Language* (Urbana, Illinois: National Council of Teachers of English 1977).

being among the most sexually stereotyped words in the language. To say that nurturing is a feminine attribute is appropriate in a discussion of Jungian archetypes, but such sexual stereotyping is not freeing to either men or women; it deepens the cultural division between women and men; and certain respectable publishing houses would find it unfit for children.

It is time to break the model of God-he. The abandonment of grammatical gender in modern American English forces religious language to alter its terminology—a move to which the church remains lamentably resistant. If increasingly in American English "he" denotes male sexuality, it becomes a simple matter of idolatry to refer to God as "he," and this is a more seminal issue than the desire to balance male with female imagery or to ascribe to God a full range of human characteristics. English-speaking linguists have long proposed options of nonsex-specific pronouns, from Charles Converse's coinage "thon" of 1859 to the contemporary suggestion of "tey-ter-tem" for subjective, possessive, and objective cases.[26] But such a pronoun change, although attractive, is unlikely in the near future, and theologians and church people are seldom in a position to effect such a change. Even granting such a change, as in the dropping of thou-thy-thee, we need a plan for the present. Let us review the options, which unfortunately are few.

The Judeo-Christian tradition of God's not being "it" is focal, and while Dionysius called the Godhead "it" with moving awe, we do not propose to refer to God as "it." "It" is used for human persons only for infants and dead bodies, and nothing suggests that "it" will be used as a nonsex-specific personal pronoun in the future.

The third singular pronoun is "she." Some people are urging that "she," which includes the word "he," be used as the generic pronoun. (It is painfully clear that the sexual connotation of any generic pronoun is of high significance, when one hears how readily this suggestion is dismissed out of hand.) If "she" were to become a generic pronoun, God would be named "she." But this is highly unlikely.

26. Casey Miller and Kate Swift, *Words and Women: New Language in New Time* (Garden City, New York: Doubleday, Anchor 1977) 116–119.

From various corners comes the suggestion that especially God the Spirit be called "she."[27] In Hebrew, spirit, *ruah*, is feminine, and some see in the Spirit's nature stereotypically feminine characteristics. But any use of "she" for God ought not be saved exclusively for God the Spirit. Assigning "he" to two persons of the Trinity and "she" to the third only further entrenches the notion of God as a sexual being. God the Spirit as "she" is unacceptable not because our God ends up only one-third female, but because we must speak of God with the highest accuracy possible, and God is neither, as modern American English knows them, he or she.

Yet there are occasions when "she" can be used metaphorically in the naming of God. Use of "she" immediately indicates the inadequacy of "he." Such metaphors occur most easily in the extended images of hymns and homilies. God the Spirit might be "she" more often than God the Son, although our tradition offers examples of the Son as Lady Wisdom and Mother Church. The appositives are already in use; we need only to extend the image to include the pronoun. Furthermore, faithfulness to God as Jesus' Abba, recital of the trinitarian creeds, and reverence to Mary as Mother of God do not imply that the first person of the Trinity is not also the mother of the faithful and the mother of creation (two very different things). However, alternate use of "he" and "she" for God in metaphoric constructions is only a partial solution, and such language always requires the Aquinas test of contradictability: God is not he, God is not she. Formal theological writing would be obscured further than it already is by an arbitrary alternation of pronouns. After all, a pronoun is meant to be a silent, unseen shorthand. Only recognition of our sexist pronoun structure forces us to focus on pronouns at all.

About the pronoun "they": contemporary grammarians realize that "they" is used regularly in spoken language as a singular generic pronoun. Some predict, even advocate, that "they" receive official singular sanction.[28] However, even if such a linguistic change would occur, "they" would not be an acceptable pronoun for God. Granting that in the Hebrew tradition one

27. For example, Jay G. Williams, "Yahweh, Women, and the Trinity," *Theology Today* 32 (1975) 240.

28. Ann Bodine, "Androcentrism in Prescriptive Grammar: singular 'they,' sex-indefinite 'he,' and 'he or she,' " *Language in Society* 4 (1975) 141.

name for God, Elohim, is plural, that plural name was assigned singular meaning. The historic stress in the Judeo-Christian tradition on monotheism forces us to reject any pronoun which connotes God as plural.

Dismissing "it" and "they," awaiting "tey," and alternating "he" with "she" is hardly a happy solution. It is incumbent upon us to eliminate altogether in American English the expository use of pronouns referring to God. A growing number of Christians for whom this is a matter of conscience regularly write and speak of God without ever using masculine pronouns. Their lectures are not clumsy nor their writings awkward. They testify that it does not take long to learn to speak and write of God without such pronoun references and that the audience remains unaware of the change. As with any translation, one cannot merely substitute one word for another. Sentences must be recast. The adjective "divine" is helpful in possessive constructions. "Godself" works well as a reflexive.[29] Its initial strangeness only adds to a healthy awe in speaking of God and a refusal to picture God as a superperson.

The issue is not whether one can speak and write with ease and clarity without calling God "he." There is ample and eloquent proof that such is possible. Rather, far too many theologians and church people refuse to take the matter seriously and make no attempt whatsoever to alter their speech. One would not mind occasional slips and would welcome a metaphoric use of "he" and "she" if there was evidence that the church was working against imaging God as male. As a result of the Black Power movement, educated Americans removed forthwith from their active vocabularies the word "Negro." Such alterations are quite possible if the motivation is present.

What is required is not only the will to change one's vocabulary, but a renewed perception of God. If we continue to think of human occupations as stereotypically male or female, then we must fight against our inclination to call a mailman "he" and a nurse "she." But when we think of human occupations as nonsex-specific, then mailcarriers and nurses are released from the categories of sex. If we again meet the God of the burning

29. For example, James F. White, *Introduction to Christian Worship* (Nashville: Abingdon 1980) 12, 18, passim.

bush, the God of the parting waters and the raining manna, the God of the wings—the mother eagle teaching her young to fly, the mother hen protecting her chicks—the God of the cross, we might be so overwhelmed by God that we laugh at the inadequacy of "he" and resolve to be more articulate in our speech. Change of speech is a willing task if it follows a conversion of mind.

The matter of translating the Bible and theological works is more difficult than the renewal of one's own speech. Of course, biblical translations must be accurate translations of the original language. But the implications of "translation" are not self-evident. How much the original concepts require translation, especially for lectionary reading, is a highly complex question. Concepts like outdated measurements—a league, a span—are usually granted contemporary substitutions without objection, but on more sensitive issues we cannot agree as to what all constitutes translation. During the next decades as some consensus in this matter is being reached, at least we can all be responsible for our own speech, and so testify both to our intent and to our understanding of how language in America functions. Meanwhile sympathetic linguists ought to proceed with the massive task of retranslating the classic library of Christian theology. Contemporarily accurate translation of theological works will rid the study of Christianity of much of its overwhelming masculine overtone.

Fortunately one genre is remarkably free from the difficulty of God-he, and that is the genre of public prayer. Liturgy, since it is in the main direct address to God, has few of the third person pronouns which cause us concern. The archaic Thou-Thy-Thee has been to great extent replaced by you-your-you, and so at least direct address to God now speaks in modern American English. So let this be our comfort: that if we are tongue-tied in preaching, speaking, and writing, we need not be so tongue-tied in praying. But our search for a new way to speak and to write makes more and more attractive the Hebraic circumlocutions for the name of God. Perhaps in the end we all will agree to write in the place of God's name only four dots and to speak for the name of God only the monk's silence.

Propositions in conclusion

1. Anthropomorphism, to the extent that it is used in the description of and naming of God, should be recognized as metaphor and must be explicated with poetic sensitivity. We should balance male with female imagery, as well as use objectification and recall the *via negativa*.

2. Human relationship terms, to the extent that they are used in the description of and naming of God, should be recognized as analogical language and must be explicated with theological sensitivity in which the revelation establishes the definition.

3. The naming of the Christian God requires a paradoxical use of human language. Human models are broken by the kerygma of the cross.

4. Masculine or feminine language used in the description of and naming of God must never imply or defend male or female sexuality in the being of God. Use of "person," as in the three persons or in God as person, must never imply inherent sexuality.

5. Modern American English is moving toward a total replacement of grammatical gender with natural gender. That is, increasingly, gender equals sexuality. To the extent that this is true, expository prose cannot refer to God as he.[30]

30. Author's note. This article was written in 1982. I stand behind its conclusion, although not its Thomistic categories of language.

20

Naming the Trinity: Orthodoxy and Inclusivity

CONSENSUS IS EMERGING WITHIN LITURGICAL CIRCLES CONCERNING inclusive language for God. Granted that current scholarly conversation has scarcely dented the impervious sacramentaries, service books, and hymnals of the land, at least one hears more and more an acknowledgment of certain linguistic principles which ought increasingly to govern the liturgical prayer of the church. Since a considerable body of literature articulating these principles is available, we need only summarily review them here: 1) human language cannot adequately express the divine; 2) yet Christians are required to speak communally; 3) religious language utilizes metaphoric speech; 4) the Judeo-Christian God has no sexuality; 5) the word *God* in contemporary American English is not a gender-specific noun; 6) Jesus is both God and a human male. More and more people are discovering ways to alter their speech and to nuance their writing in adherence to these principles so that their language comes to witness to the paradoxes of Christian speech and of an incarnate God.[1]

Yet sometimes we find ourselves back in the Arian controversy. It is not easy for human language to say all the truth about Jesus Christ in an isolated sentence. We can of course speak carefully and reverently of a God beyond sexuality, but the result of retaining masculine references for Christ is to admit a linguistic distinction which threatens the Nicene faith. Increasingly one

1. See Gail Ramshaw-Schmidt, *Christ in Sacred Speech: The Meaning of Liturgical Language* (Philadelphia: Fortress 1986).

hears that God is God and Jesus a nice man with an Abba experience, but this is not an orthodox solution to the dilemma of proclaiming the Christian faith in contemporary American English. Nicaea sought to articulate the faith that God assumed humanity so that humanity might be saved. Our task is to find language which is both orthodox—which affirms "Yes, we accept the Christian faith"—and kerygmatic—which suggests "This is how we say that faith in our tongue." Recent decades have birthed considerable exploration in God-talk, but much of the search has reflected more a stereotypical religious quest for divine imagery than an orthodox theologian's inquiry into the vernacular gospel. The most difficult question remains virtually unaddressed: is there a way to speak of the Trinity with more inclusive yet still orthodox terms?

Scholars have repeatedly demonstrated in recent decades that the Bible allows, even urges us toward, greater metaphoric possibilities in our language for God. Yet our renewed discovery of biblical imagery cannot give us license to jump from the psalms to the twentieth century. We are not back again in the first century, formulating Christianity anew. We have a history which has shaped us for better and for worse, and while we wish to redefine ourselves as distinct from the most perverse in our past, we cannot merely wish it away, if we want to remain orthodox Christians. The task of each age is to re-receive the tradition, which cannot mean to erase it; yet neither can we recite by rote the tradition as if mindless repetition constitutes orthodox kerygma.[2] The orthodox Christian God is of such a complexity that simple deity language common to all religions cannot suffice. Popular attempts at making Trinity language inclusive fall far short of what the Trinity can convey, and the resulting suggestions, although eliminating or minimizing the sexist terminology of Father and Son, substantially diminish the truths of trinitarian theology. The substitution of Parent for Father absolutely contradicts the shockingly personal revelation of God by Jesus; and somehow the Spirit must remain the Spirit of the risen Christ. "Creator, Redeemer, Sustainer" is a contemporary reincarnation of modalism which naively equates one function each to one

2. See David N. Power O.M.I., *The Sacrifice We Offer* (Edinburgh: T & T Clark 1986) 136–61, for a discussion of the contemporary interpretation of dogma.

person each, an idea wholly denied by classical theology. One person of God is not creator; "redeemer" relies on a theory of atonement which many contemporary theologians find an embarrassment; and any such three functions skirts the central Christian question in the naming of God: who is Jesus in relation to God?

The theological explication of the Trinity is a continuous task throughout church history.[3] That Trinity language has been trivialized and comes into catechesis bereft of much of its power is true. We all can cite horror stories: remember the popular ditty "Sons of God," with its couplet ". . . till we meet the Trinity, and live with them forever." But that Trinity language can be discarded is not true: Father-Son-Spirit language is normative for Christian orthodoxy. But neither is it true that the language is dead-ended in an ancient and narrow philosophical world. On the contrary, Trinity language can be seen as an astonishingly inclusive way to envision the God we know in the church.

Christian language about God begins always by asking Jesus' question, "Who do you say that I am?" The relationship between Jesus and God is the primary Christian issue, and any language which fudges on the divinity of Christ must be rejected. The answer of orthodox Christianity is that God is on the cross. As Johann Rist wrote in 1641 for a Good Friday hymn, "O grosse Not! Gott selbst ist tot," rendered unfortunately by cowardly translators as "O sorrow dread! God's Son is dead."[4] God is Jesus on the cross, between the thieves. God is there in the suffering humanity of our time. God is beyond deity language: God as master of the universe, the creative mother of paradise, the archetypal father of chauvinist society, the glorious monarch of religion. God is also Jesus Christ, a human person born, suffering, and dying. God is there in human history uniquely as the rejected and risen one. God suffers and has suffered and will suffer, and in this suffering our suffering is transformed. As well, the church attests to the relationship between the second and the first person as one of love: the God whom we imagine

3. See especially chapter 4 (83–109) in William J. Hill, *The Three-Personed God* (Washington, D.C.: Catholic University of America 1982).

4. Johann Rist, "O Darkest Woe," in W.G. Polark, *The Handbook to The Lutheran Hymnal* (St. Louis: Concordia 1958) 131.

as deity is graciously embracing the God whom we see as sufferer.

Yet we have not only a two-personed God, God as the primordial deity and God as the suffering one. The Trinity's inclusivity goes further to claim relationship beyond dualism. God is also the life of the community, the power of the Christian assembly, the animator of renewed life. Paradoxically it is the power of the suffering Christ that is transformed into the strength of the living assembly. The Christian God is not merely the God of the Twin Mountain Peaks, or the God of the Thunderclouds, or the God of Womb Waters. The Christian God is not only the usual religious God, either transcendent or immanent, either masculine or feminine, either or indeed both. The Christian God is beyond the primordial deity by being in the dying and rising Jesus of Nazareth and in the gathered and scattered eucharistic assembly. The Christian God is complex indeed; and any language which implies that God is a three-headed creature or three separate functions or three periods in history (or two males and a cloud) must be refined to speak of the deeper truth of God in Christ as deity, sufferer, and assembly.

The language used classically to reveal this triune divinity is Father-Son-Spirit. Such terminology is in the first place and of necessity biblical: theological categories are always arrangements of biblical images. Such terminology explicates the reality of Christ, as Christian language of divinity must. It is relational, corresponding to our faith that we know God not as a function fulfilled—the Being who solves a certain problem for us—but as person met—the One who loves us in the neighbor. It is easy to see why this normative language for the Trinity became nearly the sole God language used. True, the tradition has offered other images. We recall Augustine's Lover, Beloved, and Love; Catherine of Siena's "food, table, and waiter"[5] or Dante's vision in paradise of three circles of light. But Father-Son-Spirit language complemented perfectly Western Christianity's obsession with sin and forgiveness: the images for theology meshed with the prevailing anthropology, and with the Father and sin firmly en-

5. *The Prayers of Catherine of Siena*, ed. Suzanne Noffke O.P. (New York: Paulist 1983) 102.

trenched, there was scarcely room for any other images to grow. But before we can continue with the Trinity, let us examine the symbiosis between Father-Son and sin-forgiveness.

We come to know God's salvation through the kerygma of gospel preaching. Of course God and God's gift of grace are prior to human language, and thus to human categories. Yet only through word and sacrament do the faithful receive the gospel and so appropriate grace. Thus the language alive at the time of revelation is so much a part of the gospel that distinction is difficult. It is not self-evident who God is or who we are outside of biblical categories; yet even accurate translation of the original languages is problematic. That Paul speaks predominantly of the justification of sinners by a gracious God indicates not only truth about God but also the importance in first-century Palestinian Judaism of the legal metaphor describing us as convicted sinners and God as judge. Augustine and Luther help solidify this image in the theological tradition, and the model becomes the pre-eminent image in the Christian West. For this conception of God as the judging authority and of humankind as guilty offspring requiring atonement, the language of Father-Son offers an easy parallel for salvation within the life of God's very self. A stereotypical familial image functions as metaphor. The Son bears the condemnation of the sinner who offers contrition to the judging yet forgiving Father and so receives merciful life. The Father-Son language fits better with Paul's discussion of sin-forgiveness than, for example, with John's death-life. "I and the Father are one" is a much more philosophically complicated use of Father-Son language than is Luke's parable of the prodigal son or Paul's exposition of life in the Spirit. But with nearly exclusive use of the model of sin-forgiveness as the language of soteriology, Father-Son language not only became enthroned as the only container for the Christian God but also became trivialized, narrowed from what Athanasius hoped it might convey.

Yet the model of sin-forgiveness is not the only possible construct which we can extrapolate from the Scriptures and the tradition.[6] The eastern church offers an option in its preaching

6. For a full discussion of these alternate models, see Gail Ramshaw-Schmidt, "Sin: One Image of Human Limitation," *Concilium 190, The Fate of Confession*, ed. Mary Collins and David N. Power (Edinburgh: T & T Clark 1987).

of deification: the human dilemma is death, and God gives life. The human potential movement echoes the long tradition of seeing the human problem as disease and God's grace as wholeness. The liberation theologies of our century see in human oppression and injustice the greatest problem of our time, and God as calling us into a life of liberation and peace. Existential crisis, whether for Job or the contemporary philosopher, sees chaos in the self and in the world and recognizes grace in the meaning which comes by the sheer presence of God. Other models for soteriology are possible, and surely the church's freedom to use several such models is more pastorally effective, as well as more suggestive of God's fullness, than an obsessive and defensive use of only a single image.

Meditating on the diversity of ways to envision soteriology, on the richness of biblical imagery, and on the theological meaning of the Trinity, we ought to be able to discover alternate trinitarian language. Let us take the model, so prevalent in our day, of life as chaos and God as meaning. The juxtaposition of alien world cultures, the loss of accepted ethical standards, the bankruptcy of western humanism evidenced in the Holocaust: these are several demonstrations of the common contemporary experience that we live in a time of the crisis of meaning. Freedom has led back to chaos. Increasingly people find no significance in their flattened existence; many cannot discover in traditional religions a way to transform human chaos by meaning. People search for symbolic depth in shallow places. In this chaotic world, to a people hungry for meaning, the triune God is revealed as the God who transforms our search for meaning by being Emmanuel, by bearing the chaos with us. God is the *meaning* whose gracious presence calls us from doubt to faith. God has ordered primordial chaos into a fruitful garden; God speaks as Logos to the human quest; and God brings us from solipsism to community. The Scriptures are filled with stories of God's meeting people in their chaos and drawing them to divine life. Perhaps "God, the Abba, the Servant, the Paraclete" will speak some of the truth of our God to our situation of chaos.

In the naming of God, Christians begin with the reality of Jesus. It is as a servant that God comes among us as Jesus. Jesus Christ is the servant who healed broken bodies, who preached God's peace, who fed the multitudes, who bore pain for the whole people. God the Servant washed our feet and served us a meal. The servant of Isaiah's songs bears in himself the chaos of human life; this servant is a refugee from angry Herod, a lonely prophet within his religion, a victor over the final chaos of injustice and death. By being the servant Jesus, God bears within God for us the burden of human sorrow, suffering, and death. And what is the deity in relation to the suffering one? Jesus' God is Abba, the loving parent, the gracious papa, the nurturing mother, the one who hears the cry of the servant, who receives the servant in human chaos and by being there transfigures the chaos of the cross into the meaning we call resurrection. This is truly astonishing, not only that there is a God in our chaos but that God is Abba. And there is a third: the witness of Abba in the life of the Servant is Paraclete. God the Paraclete is the comforter for the community's pain, the counselor for the assembly's quest, their advocate before the world's chaos.

Modern English remembers its Judeo-Christian linguistic roots in its contemporary expression: *Abba* is Aramaic, *Paraclete* Greek, and *Servant* Latin, the various strains of our tradition cooperating to attest to a God faithful within chaotic human history. Abba is the loving deity of all time, who saved Noah, who restored Job, who led Israel by a pillar of fire as they wandered lost in the desert, who joined the three men in the fiery furnace, who received the plea of the crucified, and who accepts our intercessory prayers. Servant is God in the suffering of Jesus and in the suffering of the world's present crises. Servant is God offering God's very self for our food. Elie Wiesel narrates the crux of the Christian faith in his tale of watching the Jewish boy hanging, that boy too frail and light for the hanging to bring on death: "Where is God now? . . . Where is He? Here He is—He is hanging here on this gallows."[7] And this is gospel, unbelievable good news, that God the Servant has been hanged with us and for us; that if we must live and die within such an absence of meaning, meaning can come from God-with-us. Paraclete is God in the assembly, the renewed community. Paraclete is the hope within the baptized, who are called into meaning and so, by their love for one another and for the world, give the meaning of the Abba to a chaotic time.

7. Elie Wiesel, *Night*, tr. Stella Rodway (New York: Bantam 1960) 62.

The language of God, the Abba, the Servant, the Paraclete, is of course not meant to replace classic trinitarian language. Rather, models such as Abba-Servant-Paraclete can complement our normative imagery of the triune God. Such language can assist preaching and teaching, especially when texts like the slaughter of the innocents, the persecution of the faithful, the rejection of Jesus, or the suffering of the just beg for imagery deeper than sin-forgiveness. Some lessons fit uniquely well with God as Abba, Servant, Paraclete. Recall the readings in Isaiah 42 and Acts 10 on the Baptism of our Lord, and consider such a prayer as this:

> O God, our Abba, gracious and good,
> you have come among us as the Servant,
> healing our wounds, bringing forth justice,
> and enlightening the earth's dark places.
> Renew us by our baptism,
> that with your Paraclete alive in us,
> we may serve all the world with your justice and love;
> through Jesus Christ, your beloved one,
> who lives and reigns with you in the Paraclete,
> one God, now and forever.

The common doxology can be cast in the following way:

> Praise God, the Abba bearing love;
> Praise God, the Servant from above;
> Praise God, the Paraclete we share:
> O triune God, receive our prayer.

The following can be used as a blessing:

> May God the Abba embrace you in love forever;
> may God the Servant bear your burdens in your place;
> may God the Paraclete grant you life with one another:
> so may the blessing of God,
> the Abba, the Servant, the Paraclete,
> be with you always.

Liturgical prayer is the entry of the community into the life of God. Standing as the Servant, the Paraclete cries out through the church to the Abba for the meaning without which life is only a waiting for death. As we pray to God, the Abba, the Servant, the Paraclete, we insert our very assembly into the triune God. Not only does our prayer go to God; in our praying we find ourselves in God, the God who is dying to include us all in divine life, the God who is Abba and Servant and Paraclete. If our current descriptions of the orthodox Trinity do not convey our assemblies of prayer into God's life, surely other biblical language than Father-Son-Spirit can assist us, that we may be propelled into that God praised by the New Testament writers, the Cappadocians, and contemporary Americans alike. Inclusive language may be a new idea, but inclusivity is the deepest truth of the triune God. Let us work together toward this goal, that we find the words to dance around that God of both Nicaea and New York City, of both orthodoxy and inclusivity.

BV 178 .R35 1988
Ramshaw, Gail
Worship